TEACHER'S PET PUBLICATIONS

LITPLAN TEACHER PACK
for
Bud, Not Buddy
based on the book by
Christopher Paul Curtis

Written by
Mary B. Collins

© 2003 Teacher's Pet Publications
All Rights Reserved

This **LitPlan** for Christopher Paul Curtis's
Bud, Not Buddy
has been brought to you by Teacher's Pet Publications, Inc.

Copyright Teacher's Pet Publications 2003
11504 Hammock Point
Berlin MD 21811

Only the student materials in this unit plan (such as worksheets,
study questions, and tests) may be reproduced multiple times
for use in the purchaser's classroom.

For any additional copyright questions,
contact Teacher's Pet Publications.

www.tpet.com

TABLE OF CONTENTS - *Bud, Not Buddy*

Introduction	5
Unit Objectives	7
Reading Assignment Sheet	8
Unit Outline	9
Study Questions (Short Answer)	13
Quiz/Study Questions (Multiple Choice)	30
Pre-reading Vocabulary Worksheets	55
Lesson One (Introductory Lesson)	69
Nonfiction Assignment Sheet	71
Oral Reading Evaluation Form	90
Writing Assignment 1	80
Writing Assignment 2	84
Writing Assignment 3	91
Vocabulary Review Activities	100
Extra Writing Assignments/Discussion ?s	95
Unit Review Activities	102
Unit Tests	105
Unit Resource Materials	151
Vocabulary Resource Materials	175

A FEW NOTES ABOUT THE AUTHOR
Christopher Paul Curtis

Christopher Paul Curtis was born and raised in Flint, Michigan (the setting for *Bud, Not Buddy*). After graduating from school, he worked on the assembly line of the Fisher Body Flint Plant 1 until his wife suggested that he "better hurry up and start doing something constructive" with his life, at which time he began his writing career.

Mr. Curtis attended the University of Michigan and won the Avery Hopwood Prize as well as the Jules Hopwood Prize for some of his writing there.

Mr. Curtis's major publications include *The Watsons Go to Birmingham 1963* (Newbery Honor and Coretta Scott King Honor) and *Bud, Not Buddy* (Newbery Medal, Coretta Scott King Award).

Windsor, Ontario, Canada is his current home, where he lives with his wife Kaysandra and children Steven Darrell and Cydney McKenzie. His real-life grandfathers were Earl "Lefty" Lewis, a Negro Baseball League pitcher, and Herman E. Curtis, Sr., a 1930's bandleader of "Herman Curtis and the Dusky Devastators of the Depression."

INTRODUCTION

This unit has been designed to develop students' reading, writing, thinking, and language skills through exercises and activities related to *Bud, Not Buddy* by Christopher Paul Curtis. It includes twenty lessons, supported by extra resource materials.

In the **introductory lesson** students are given the materials they will be using during the unit. At the end of the lesson, students begin the pre-reading work for the first reading assignment.

In addition, there is a **nonfiction reading assignment**. Students are required to read two pieces of nonfiction related in some way to *Bud, Not Buddy*. After reading their nonfiction pieces, students will fill out a worksheet on which they answer questions regarding facts, interpretation, criticism, and personal opinions. During two class periods, students make **oral presentations** about the nonfiction pieces they have read. This not only exposes all students to a wealth of information, it also gives students the opportunity to practice **public speaking**.

The **reading assignments** are approximately thirty pages each; some are a little shorter while others are a little longer. Students have approximately 15 minutes of pre-reading work to do prior to each reading assignment. This pre-reading work involves reviewing the study questions for the assignment and doing some vocabulary work for 8 to 10 vocabulary words they will encounter in their reading.

The **study guide questions** are fact-based questions; students can find the answers to these questions right in the text. These questions come in two formats: short answer required or multiple choice. The best use of these materials is probably to use the short answer version of the questions as study guides for students (since answers will be more complete), and to use the multiple choice version for occasional quizzes. If your school has the appropriate equipment, it might be a good idea to make transparencies of your answer keys for the overhead projector.

The **vocabulary work** is intended to enrich students' vocabularies as well as to aid in the students' understanding of the book. Prior to each reading assignment, students will complete a two-part worksheet for several vocabulary words in the upcoming reading assignment. Part I focuses on students' use of general knowledge and contextual clues by giving the sentence in which the word appears in the text. Students are then to write down what they think the words mean based on the words' usage. Part II nails down the definitions of the words by giving students dictionary definitions of the words and having students match the words to the correct definitions based on the words' contextual usage. Students should then have an understanding of the words when they meet them in the text.

After each reading assignment, students will go back and formulate answers for the study guide questions. Discussion of these questions serves as a **review** of the most important events and ideas presented in the reading assignments.

After students complete reading the work, there is a **vocabulary review** lesson which pulls together all of the fragmented vocabulary lists for the reading assignments and gives students a review of all of the words they have studied.

A lesson is devoted to the **extra discussion questions/writing assignments**. These questions focus on interpretation, critical analysis and personal response, employing a variety of thinking skills and adding to the students' understanding of the novel.

The **group activity** which follows the discussion questions has students working together to create a film about China using all the information they have gathered through the nonfiction reading assignment, the reading and discussion of the book, and the writing assignments.

There are three **writing assignments** in this unit, each with the purpose of informing, persuading, or having students express personal opinions. The first assignment is **to express personal opinions** about the meaning of the sign at the mission. The second assignment is **to inform**: students are each assigned one of the factual people, places or things Bud mentions in the book to research. The third assignment is **to persuade**: students choose a point of view regarding either the incident with the Amoses or the incident at the train and write a persuasive argument supporting the position they believe is correct.

The **review lesson** pulls together all of the aspects of the unit. The teacher is given four or five choices of activities or games to use which all serve the same basic function of reviewing all of the information presented in the unit.

The **unit test** comes in two formats: all multiple choice-matching-true/false or with a mixture of matching, short answer, multiple choice, and composition. As a convenience, two different tests for each format have been included.

There are additional **support materials** included with this unit. The **Resource Materials** sections include suggestions for an in-class library, crossword and word search puzzles related to the novel, and extra vocabulary worksheets. There is a list of **bulletin board ideas** which gives the teacher suggestions for bulletin boards to go along with this unit. In addition, there is a list of **extra class activities** the teacher could choose from to enhance the unit or as a substitution for an exercise the teacher might feel is inappropriate for his/her class. **Answer keys** are located directly after the **reproducible student materials** throughout the unit. Only the student materials may be reproduced for use in the teacher's classroom without infringement of copyrights.

UNIT OBJECTIVES - *Bud, Not Buddy*

1. Students will answer questions to demonstrate their knowledge and understanding of the main events and characters in *Bud, Not Buddy* as they relate to the author's theme development.

2. Students will demonstrate their understanding of the text on four levels: factual, interpretive, critical, and personal.

3. Students will study the main symbols used in the novel, including the suitcase, doors opening and closing, Bud's blanket, and others.

4. Students will discuss the idea of equality and morality as it relates to race issues; the prevalent idea in this book that just because some people are homeless or poor doesn't mean that they are bad people. There are good people and bad people in all races.

5. Students will be given the opportunity to practice reading aloud and silently to improve their skills in each area.

6. Students will research and discuss the names of real people, places and things mentioned in the book: Al Capone, John Brown, Herbert Hoover, and others.

7. Students will enrich their vocabularies and improve their understanding of the novel through the vocabulary lessons prepared for use in conjunction with the novel.

8. The writing assignments in this unit are geared to several purposes:
    a. To have students demonstrate their abilities to inform, to persuade, or to express their own personal ideas
        NOTE: Students will demonstrate ability to write effectively to <u>inform</u> by developing and organizing facts to convey information. Students will demonstrate the ability to write effectively to <u>persuade</u> by selecting and organizing relevant information, establishing an argumentative purpose, and by designing an appropriate strategy for an identified audience. Students will demonstrate the ability to write effectively to <u>express personal ideas</u> by selecting a form and its appropriate elements.
    b. To check the students' reading comprehension
    c. To make students think about the ideas presented by the novel
    d. To encourage logical thinking
    e. To provide an opportunity to practice good grammar and improve students' use of the English language.

9. Students will read aloud, report, and participate in large and small group discussions to improve their public speaking and personal interaction skills.

READING ASSIGNMENT SHEET - *Bud, Not Buddy*

Date Assigned	Chapters Assigned	Completion Date
	1-2	
	3-5	
	6-7	
	8	
	9-10	
	11	
	12-13	
	14-15	
	16-18	
	19	

UNIT OUTLINE - *Bud, Not Buddy*

1 Introduction PVR 1-2	2 Study ?s 1-2 Group Work PVR 3-5	3 Study ?s 3-5 PVR 6-7	4 Study ?s 6-7 Group Work Assign PVR 8	5 Study ?s 8 Writing Assignment 1 PVR 9-10
6 Study ?s 9-10 PVR 11	7 Study ?s 11 Writing Assignment 2 PVR 12-13	8 Study ?s 12-13 PVR 14-15	9 Study ?s 14-15 PVR16-18 Group Work	10 Study?s 16-18 PVR19
11 Study?s 19 Writing Assignment 3	12 Group Work	13 Reports/Discuss	14 Reports/Discuss	15 Reports/Discuss
16 Extra Discussion Questions	17 Extra Discussion Questions	18 Vocab Review	19 Unit Review	20 Unit Test

Key: P=Preview Study Questions V=Prereading Vocabulary Worksheet R=Read

STUDY GUIDE QUESTIONS

SHORT ANSWER STUDY GUIDE QUESTIONS - *Bud, Not Buddy*

Chapter 1
1. What good news did Bud and Jerry get?
2. According to Bud, did he have a better foster family assignment than Jerry did? Explain.
3. Why is six a tough age?
4. What was printed on the blue flyer? Why was it special?

Chapter 2
1. Identify Todd Amos.
2. What promise did Mr. and Mrs. Amos break?
3. What warnings did Todd give Bud about the shed?

Chapter 3
1. What were the door knob guards in the shed?
2. How did "Bugs" get his nickname?
3. What was the vampire bat?
4. Why did Bud get mad after he got out of the shed?

Chapter 4
1. Why was the first part of Bud's revenge plan to get the gun out of the way?
2. What was part two of Bud's revenge plan?

Chapter 5
1. Where did Bud go when he left the Amoses?
2. What did Bud's use of his blanket tell us about him?
3. Why was Momma unhappy in the picture taken at the Miss B. Gotten Moon Park?
4. What did Momma tell Bud about his name?
5. What did Momma tell Bud about doors?

Chapter 6
1. Who was Clarence?
2. What did Bud's pretend mother and daddy do that annoyed him?
3. What did the sign hanging over the building at the mission say?

Chapter 7
1. What happened to Miss Hill, the librarian?
2. What did the other librarian show Bud?
3. What did Bud know about the library door's closing?

Bud, Not Buddy Short Answer Study Questions page 2

Chapter 8
1. Who attacked Bud under the tree at the library?
2. What did Bugs and Bud decide to do?
3. Why was "Hooperville" so hard to find?
4. How did Bugs rig the coin toss?
5. How did "Hooverville" get its name?
6. What kind of a welcome did the boys get at Hooverville?
7. What promise did the Hooverville woman make to Bud when she told him to leave his bags while he did the dishes? Did she keep the promise?
8. Who was Deza Malone?
9. What was Bud's reply when Deza said, ". . . But you have been staying in an orphanage"?
10. Why did *Shenandoah* remind Deza of her mother and father?
11. Why did Deza feel sorry for the people with the sick baby?
12. Why did Bud start wondering if going to California was the right thing to do?
13. What did the smell of Bud's blanket remind him of?
14. Why did Bud try to fall asleep before Momma was done reading the story at night?
15. What caused Bud to jump straight up and bang his head on the top of the shack?
16. Why did Bud miss the train?
17. Why did the police try to stop the people from getting on the train?
18. What happened to Hooverville?
19. What good things came out of Bud's trip to Hooverville?
20. What did Bud realize about the names Caldwell and Calloway?

Chapter 9
1. Where did Bud go after breakfast at the mission? Why?
2. Why did Bud like Civil War books?
3. How are ideas like seeds?
4. How did Bud get the idea that Herman E. Calloway might be his father?
5. Why did Bud decide to walk across the state of Michigan from Flint to Grand Rapids?

Chapter 10
1. What kid-like thing did Bud do when he came to the sign that marked the city limits of Flint?
2. How did the man know that Bud was from Flint and was hungry?
3. Why did Bud tell the man he had run away from Grand Rapids?
4. Why did Bud try to drive away the man's car?

Bud, Not Buddy Short Answer Study Questions page 3

Chapter 11
1. Why did Bud say that it's terrible to have been brought up proper?
2. Why did Bud insist on seeing the man's teeth?
3. Who was Lefty Lewis?
4. How did Bud know he was going to be safe?
5. Why did Bud sleep so well in the car and through that first night with Mr. Lewis?
6. Why did Bud pretend to still be asleep even though he was awake?
7. Who was Mrs. Sleet?
8. What was Bud's reason for thinking it was okay to lie to an adult but not to a kid?
9. How was mealtime at the Sleets' house different from mealtime at the home?
10. Who were "redcaps"?

Chapter 12
1. How is a telegram different from a regular letter?
2. Why did the policeman stop Lefty and search the car?
3. Why did Bud at first say he didn't think he needed to see what was in the box in Lefty's car?
4. What was in the box in Lefty's car the day the policeman stopped him?
5. Why would the workers go on a "sit down" strike instead of a regular strike?
6. Why didn't Bud want Mr. Lewis to talk to Herman E. Calloway?
7. Why did Lefty tell Bud to come see him if he decided to travel again?
8. What immediate proof did Bud get that HEC was his father? What words did he use?
9. What made Bud's "maple tree" shake in the wind?
10. Why did Bud think he wasn't a "regular kid"?

Chapter 13
1. What was Bud's first impression of Herman E. Calloway?
2. Match the person with their instrument.
   ___ Doug "The Thug" Tennant   A. trombone
   ___ "Steady" Eddie Patrick   B. piano
   ___ Chug "Doo-Doo-Bug" Cross   C. drums
   ___ Roy "Dirty Deed" Breed   D. saxophone

3. Why did Bud slap his hand over his mouth?
4. Why was Steady Eddie Bud's favorite?
5. Identify *Sweet Pea*.

Bud, Not Buddy Short Answer Study Questions page 4

Chapter 14
1. Who is Miss Thomas?
2. What hit Bud as hard as Snaggletooth MacNevin had smacked Herman E. Calloway?
3. What did Bud decide when he realized that this is where he was supposed to be?
4. Why did Bud cry?

Chapter 15
1. What was Grand Calloway Station?
2. What scared Bud the most when Miss Thomas showed him his room?
3. What warning did Herman E. Calloway give Bud about snooping around the house?
4. What was Bud's reaction to Herman E. Calloway's warning?

Chapter 16
1. Why did Bud's eyes get all sting-y when he looked at his clothes in the morning?
2. Why did Bud make so much noise when he came downstairs?
3. What did the band, Mr. Calloway and Miss Thomas decide about Bud while he slept that first night?
4. What did Steady Eddie give Bud? What might it symbolize?
5. What name did Bud get? Why?

Chapter 17
1. Why was Herman E. Calloway doing a bad job of making Bud work like a dog?
2. What did Bud say the band should be called?

Chapter 18
1. What were the band members' favorite things to do, according to Bud?
2. What was the answer to Bud's question, "Why does he always keep one white guy in the band?"
3. What unhappy news did Bud get when he was packing up at the Laughing Jackass?
4. What finally convinced Herman E. Calloway that Bud might be his relative?

Bud, Not Buddy Short Answer Study Questions page 5

Chapter 19
1. What did Bud see that made his heart jump down into his stomach when he went upstairs to get the pictures?
2. What was Herman E. Calloway trying to say to Bud when Bud touched him while they were in the dead girl's room?
3. What was the final proof that Bud was related to Herman E. Calloway?
4. What did Bud realize about the dead girl's room?
5. What was so special about the picture that Miss Thomas gave Bud?
6. What was written on the stones, and why was it written on them?
7. What did Miss Thomas ask Bud to be?
8. What did the guys in the band buy for Bud?
9. What was funny about Bud saying he would play his saxophone as well as the other band members played their instruments in about three weeks?
10. What did Bud put in Herman E. Calloway's room? Why?
11. Why did Bud put his mother's Miss B. Gotten Moon Park picture on the wall?
12. Why didn't Bud need his suitcase items anymore?
13. What did the squeaks and squawks of the saxophone sound like to Bud?

ANSWER KEY: SHORT ANSWER STUDY GUIDE QUESTIONS - *Bud, Not Buddy*

Chapter 1

1. What good news did Bud and Jerry get?
   They were going to foster homes.

2. According to Bud, did he have a better foster family assignment than Jerry did? Explain.
   No. He said, "I know being in a house with three girls sounds terrible, Jerry, but it's a lot better than being with a boy who's a couple of years older than you. . . . A older boy is going to want to fight, but those little girls are going to treat you real good."

3. Why is six a tough age?
   "It's at six that grown folks don't think you're a cute little kid anymore, they talk to you and expect that you understand everything they mean . . . it's around six that grown folks stop giving you little swats and taps and jump clean up to giving you slugs that'll knock you right down. . . . Six is a bad time too 'cause that's when scary things start to happen to your body, it's around then that your teeth start coming a-loose in your mouth." Bud was six when his mother died, and he was sent to the home.

4. What was printed on the blue flyer? Why was it special?
   The paper was a flyer advertising Herman E. Calloway and the Dusky Devastators of the Depression, with a picture of a man standing next to a giant fiddle. Bud thought the man might be his father.

Chapter 2

1. Identify Todd Amos.
   Todd was the spirited son of Mr. and Mrs. Amos, who provided a foster home for Bud. Todd shoved a pencil up Bud's nose. Bud hit him and Todd beat up Bud, blaming the incident on him.

2. What promise did Mr. and Mrs. Amos break?
   They said they would not look in his suitcase, but they did.

3. What warnings did Todd give Bud about the shed?
   Todd warned Bud of vampire bats, spiders and centipedes. He said that the last kid in there got stung, and the kid before that was not found; there was just a puddle of blood.

Bud, Not Buddy Short Answer Study Question Key page 2

Chapter 3

1. What were the door knob guards in the shed?
    They were dried out fish heads someone had nailed to the door.

2. How did "Bugs" get his nickname?
    A cockroach crawled into his ear one night.

3. What was the vampire bat?
    It was a hornets' nest.

4. Why did Bud get mad after he got out of the shed?
    He was mad at the Amos family but mostly mad at himself for believing there was a vampire in the shed and for getting trapped in a situation where there wasn't anyone who cared what happened to him.

Chapter 4

1. Why was the first part of Bud's revenge plan to get the gun out of the way?
    If something went wrong with the revenge plan, he didn't want the Amoses to get the gun and shoot him.

2. What was part two of Bud's revenge plan?
    He poured water on Todd's pajama pants while Todd was sleeping, inducing the desired effect–Todd's wetting the bed.

Chapter 5

1. Where did Bud go when he left the Amoses?
    He went to the library to sleep in the basement and get advice from Miss Hill.

2. What did Bud's use of his blanket tell us about him?
    First, he's smart enough to recognize the value of a blanket and to carry one with him. Also, that he folds it neatly in his suitcase to keep things in place shows us he is smart, neat and careful with his things.

3. Why was Momma unhappy in the picture taken at the Miss B. Gotten Moon Park?
    Her father made her get the picture taken with that filthy hat on.

Bud, Not Buddy Short Answer Study Question Key page 3

4. What did Momma tell Bud about his name?
    She told him she named him Bud, not Buddy. "A bud is a flower-to-be. A flower in waiting. Waiting for just the right warmth and care to open it up. A little fist of love waiting to unfold and be seen by the world."

5. What did Momma tell Bud about doors?
    "No matter how bad things look to you, no matter how dark the night, when one door closes, don't worry, because another door opens."

Chapter 6

1. Who was Clarence?
    Bud was Clarence. The kind people at the mission made up a name to call him to help him get into the mission for food.

2. What did Bud's pretend mother and daddy do that annoyed him?
    They kept smacking him in the back of the head. Also, he wished they had picked another name besides "Clarence" for him.

3. What did the sign hanging over the building at the mission say?
    "There's no place like America today!"

Chapter 7

1. What happened to Miss Hill, the librarian?
    She got married and moved to Chicago.

2. What did the other librarian show Bud?
    She showed him how to look in the mileage guide to calculate how far it was from Flint to Chicago, then how to calculate how long it would take to get there walking.

3. What did Bud know about the library door's closing?
    "That library door closing after I walked out was the exact kind of door Momma had told me about. I knew that since it had closed the next one was about to open."

Bud, Not Buddy Short Answer Study Question Key page 4

Chapter 8

1. Who attacked Bud under the tree at the library?
    Bugs did.

2. What did Bugs and Bud decide to do?
    They were going to hop on trains and ride them west, to go pick fruit out there and make money to live on.

3. Why was "Hooperville" so hard to find?
    Actually it was a "Hooverville," just a little settlement of make-shift shacks that homeless people put up.

4. How did Bugs rig the coin toss?
    He said, "Heads I win, tails you lose." Bugs would win either way.

5. How did "Hooverville" get its name?
    It was named after President Hoover. The residents of Hoovervilles blamed him for the bad economy which made them jobless and homeless.

6. What kind of a welcome did the boys get at Hooverville?
    They got a warm welcome from the people there. There was a fire and music, and the boys were invited to share dinner with the residents.

7. What promise did the Hooverville woman make to Bud when she told him to leave his bags while he did the dishes? Did she keep the promise?
    She told him his suitcase would be safe; no one would look inside of it. She did keep the promise.

8. Who was Deza Malone?
    She was the girl at Hooverville who washed dishes with Bud, talked with him, and kissed him.

9. What was Bud's reply when Deza said, ". . . But you have been staying in an orphanage"?
    Bud said, "I been staying in a home."

10. Why did *Shenandoah* remind Deza of her mother and father?
    The song's verse was about an Indian man and woman who had been apart for seven years but were still in love. Deza knows that even though her parents are separated, they still love each other.

Bud, Not Buddy Short Answer Study Question Key page 5

11. Why did Deza feel sorry for the people with the sick baby?
    They were too proud to accept help from people they thought were beneath their station in life.

12. Why did Bud start wondering if going to California was the right thing to do?
    He was thinking that "Deza's momma was right, someone who doesn't know who their family is, is like dust blowing around in a storm. . . ." He thought it was more likely he could find his own family closer to Flint than in California.

13. What did the smell of Bud's blanket remind him of?
    It reminded him of Momma and how she used to read him to sleep every night.

14. Why did Bud try to fall asleep before Momma was done reading the story at night?
    He didn't want to have to listen to the explanation of what the story was about. He thought the explanation took all the fun out of the story.

15. What caused Bud to jump straight up and bang his head on the top of the shack?
    A man was screaming at the top of his lungs for everyone to get up, that the train was leaving early.

16. Why did Bud miss the train?
    He ran back to get his blue flyer he had left at the shack in Hooverville. When he returned and tried to catch the train, he threw the suitcase to Bugs, but the blue flyer he had hastily slipped under the twine on his suitcase fell out. Bud stopped to get it and put it in his pocket, and the delay was just enough to keep him from being able to catch the train.

17. Why did the police try to stop the people from getting on the train?
    None of them had tickets.

18. What happened to Hooverville?
    The police tore it down and burned it.

19. What good things came out of Bud's trip to Hooverville?
    He kissed a girl and stayed in Flint.

20. What did Bud realize about the names Caldwell and Calloway?
    He noticed that "both of them have eight letters and there aren't too many names that have a C, a A, a L, and a W all together like that. . . . a good criminal chooses a alias that's kind of close to their own name.

Bud, Not Buddy Short Answer Study Question Key page 6

Chapter 9

1. Where did Bud go after breakfast at the mission? Why?
   He went to the library to see how far it was from Flint to Grand Rapids so he could calculate how long it would take him to walk there to find Herman E. Calloway.

2. Why did Bud like Civil War books?
   They had "the best gory pictures in the world."

3. How are ideas like seeds?
   "Both of them start real, real small and then . . . woop, zoop, sloop . . . before you can say Jack Robinson they've gone and grown a lot bigger than you ever thought they could."

4. How did Bud get the idea that Herman E. Calloway might be his father?
   Billy Burns at the orphanage bet Bud a nickel he didn't even know who his father was. Before he thought, Bud blurted out that his dad played a giant fiddle and was named Herman E. Calloway.

5. Why did Bud decide to walk across the state of Michigan from Flint to Grand Rapids?
   Bud's idea that Herman E. Calloway was his father grew and grew until, finally, Bud decided to go to Grand Rapids to find him.

Chapter 10

1. What kid-like thing did Bud do when he came to the sign that marked the city limits of Flint?
   He "jumped in and out of Flint seven times" before he went on towards Grand Rapids.

2. How did the man know that Bud was from Flint and was hungry?
   Flint was the closest town, so it would be a good guess that a small boy would be from the nearest city. Also, Bud was small, and if he were running away from home, he probably was hungry.

3. Why did Bud tell the man he had run away from Grand Rapids?
   Bud knew that if he told the man he was from Flint, the man would take him back to Flint. Bud wanted to go to Grand Rapids, so he thought that if he told the man he was from Grand Rapids, the man would take him there.

4. Why did Bud try to drive away the man's car?
   He saw the box of blood on the car seat and thought the man was a vampire.

Bud, Not Buddy Short Answer Study Question Key page 7

Chapter 11

1. Why did Bud say that it's terrible to have been brought up proper?
    When the grown-up man told him to roll down the window, he did it out of obedience to the grown-up.

2. Why did Bud insist on seeing the man's teeth?
    The arguments the man was making, saying he was not a vampire, were logical. Bud was being cautious and making sure by seeing the man's teeth.

3. Who was Lefty Lewis?
    He was the man who stopped to pick up Bud on the road between Flint and Oswego.

4. How did Bud know he was going to be safe?
    He had "never heard of a vampire that could drive a car and had never seen one that had such a good sense of humor."

5. Why did Bud sleep so well in the car and through that first night with Mr. Lewis?
    He felt safe with someone who cared about him and would take him to Herman E. Calloway. He could relax.

6. Why did Bud pretend to still be asleep even though he was awake?
    He wasn't sure where he was, and he wanted to find out as much as he could from the conversations going on around him before the people knew he was awake.

7. Who was Mrs. Sleet?
    She was Lefty's daughter.

8. What was Bud's reason for thinking it was okay to lie to an adult but not to a kid?
    "Most times adults want to hear something that lets them take their attention off you and put it on something else. That makes it easy and not too bad to lie to them. . . . Most times kids really do want to know what they're asking you." So it would be more wrong to lie to someone who really wants to know.

9. How was mealtime at the Sleets' house different from mealtime at the home?
    At the home, the boys were not allowed to talk at all during meals. The Sleets talked continuously through the meal.

10. Who were "redcaps"?
    They were the men at the railroad station who loaded the trains and took people's bags to their cars.

Bud, Not Buddy Short Answer Study Question Key page 8

Chapter 12

1. How is a telegram different from a regular letter?
    You have to pay for each letter, so you try to say what you have to say with as few letters as possible. Instead of periods at the end of each thought, the telegram code is "stop."

2. Why did the policeman stop Lefty and search the car?
    He was looking for labor organizers who were stirring up trouble in the factories.

3. Why did Bud at first say he didn't think he needed to see what was in the box in Lefty's car?
    He sensed he would be better off not knowing.

4. What was in the box in Lefty's car the day the policeman stopped him?
    There were flyers announcing a meeting for the newly formed Grand Rapids Branch of the Brotherhood of Pullman Porters–a meeting for organizing workers into a union.

5. Why would the workers go on a "sit down" strike instead of a regular strike?
    If they left their posts, the employers would simply hire new workers to replace them.

6. Why didn't Bud want Mr. Lewis to talk to Herman E. Calloway?
    He had lied to Mr. Lewis, and he couldn't let the two talk before he figured things out; he knew he'd be on the first transportation available back to Flint.

7. Why did Lefty tell Bud to come see him if he decided to travel again?
    He liked Bud and would want to take care of him so no harm would come to him.

8. What immediate proof did Bud get that HEC was his father? What words did he use?
    Bud thought HEC was talking just like him. He said, "There comes a time when you're doing something and you realize it just doesn't make sense to keep on doing it, you ain't being a quitter, it's just that the good Lord has seen fit to give you the sense to know, you understand, enough is enough."

9. What made Bud's "maple tree" shake in the wind?
    Herman E. Calloway was old–really old. Maybe too old to be his father.

10. Why did Bud think he wasn't a "regular kid"?
    "I knew if I was a regular kid I'd be crying buckets of tears now."

Bud, Not Buddy Short Answer Study Question Key page 9

Chapter 13

1. What was Bud's first impression of Herman E. Calloway?
    He "seemed like he was going to be hard to get along with."

2. Match the person with their instrument.
    ___ Doug "The Thug"Tennant   A. trombone
    ___ "Steady" Eddie Patrick   B. piano
    ___ Chug "Doo-Doo-Bug" Cross C. drums
    ___ Roy "Dirty Deed" Breed   D. saxophone

3. Why did Bud slap his hand over his mouth?
    He was disrespectful, calling Herman E. Calloway a mean, old coot. It was out before he thought, and he reacted by slapping his hand over his mouth as soon as he realized what he had done.

4. Why was Steady Eddie Bud's favorite?
    Eddie was clearly on Bud's side and was looking out for him.

5. Identify *Sweet Pea*.
    It was the restaurant HEC's band frequented.

Chapter 14

1. Who is Miss Thomas?
    Miss Thomas was the band's vocalist. She apparently had a special relationship with Herman E. Calloway. She helped take care of Bud.

2. What hit Bud as hard as Snaggletooth MacNevin had smacked Herman E. Calloway?
    "All of a sudden I knew that of all the places in the world that I'd ever been in this was the one. That of all the people I'd ever met these were the ones. This was where I was supposed to be."

3. What did Bud decide when he realized that this is where he was supposed to be?
    He decided it would take a lot more than a "grouchy, old, bald-headed guy with a tremendous belly to run" him out of there.

4. Why did Bud cry?
    He was happy and relieved to be home.

Bud, Not Buddy Short Answer Study Question Key page 10

Chapter 15

1. What was Grand Calloway Station?
    It was Mr. Calloway's home where Mr. Calloway, Miss Thomas, and Bud stayed.

2. What scared Bud the most when Miss Thomas showed him his room?
    "Those two little doors were starting to make me nervous. They looked like they were just right for a young Frankenstein or wolfman to come busting out of once all the grown folks left the room. . . ."

3. What warning did Herman E. Calloway give Bud about snooping around the house?
    "I know where every single thing belongs and I can tell right away when something's missing. I've got little secret bells all over everything and when something's stolen the bell goes off and only I can hear it, so watch your step."

4. What was Bud's reaction to Herman E. Calloway's warning?
    ". . . nothing makes you want to steal something more than having somebody who doesn't even know you're honest telling you not to steal. Herman E. Calloway didn't have to worry, I was a liar, not a thief."

Chapter 16

1. Why did Bud's eyes get all sting-y when he looked at his clothes in the morning?
    They were folded like his mother folded them before she went to work in the mornings. He was thinking about his mother.

2. Why did Bud make so much noise when he came downstairs?
    He wanted everyone to know he was coming. He had heard them talking about him, and he wanted to give them warning he was coming so they wouldn't be saying something they didn't want him to hear as he came in the room.

3. What did the band, Mr. Calloway and Miss Thomas decide about Bud while he slept that first night?
    They decided they would let him stay at Grand Calloway Station for a while.

4. What did Steady Eddie give Bud? What might it symbolize?
    He gave Bud a saxophone case to use as a new suitcase. He carried his life around in his old suitcase, so perhaps the saxophone case symbolizes his new life.

5. What name did Bud get? Why?
    Bud's band name was Sleepy LaBone because he slept so late in the morning and he was skinny.

Bud, Not Buddy Short Answer Study Question Key page 11

Chapter 17

1. Why was Herman E. Calloway doing a bad job of making Bud work like a dog?
    Bud was enjoying it!

2. What did Bud say the band should be called?
    He said it should be called Miss Thomas and the Dusky Devastators of the Depression and a Mean Old Guy on the Giant Fiddle.

Chapter 18

1. What were the band members' favorite things to do, according to Bud?
    The band liked to play music, tease each other, and talk about Herman E. Calloway behind his back.

2. What was the answer to Bud's question, "Why does he always keep one white guy in the band?"
    It was against the law for a Negro to own property where the Log Cabin is, so Mr. Calloway put it in Deed's name. Also, Eddie explained that, ". . . a lot of times we get gigs playing polkas and waltzes and a lot of these white folks wouldn't hire us if they knew we were a Negro band so Deed goes out and sets up everything."

3. What unhappy news did Bud get when he was packing up at the Laughing Jackass?
    He had to ride home with Herman E. Calloway.

4. What finally convinced Herman E. Calloway that Bud might be his relative?
    Bud produced the stones that Herman Calloway had sent to Bud's mother, HEC's daughter.

Chapter 19

1. What did Bud see that made his heart jump down into his stomach when he went upstairs to get the pictures?
    He saw Herman E. Calloway sitting on the little chair in front of the little mirror on the dressing table. His elbows were on the table and his face was covered by his hands. It sounded like he was having trouble breathing 'cause every time he sucked in a bunch of air he made a sound like, "Mu-u-u-u-h" and every time he blew air out he made a sound like, "H-u-u-u-h."

2. What was Herman E. Calloway trying to say to Bud when Bud touched him while they were in the dead girl's room?
    He was trying to say he was sorry.

Bud, Not Buddy Short Answer Study Question Key page 12

3. What was the final proof that Bud was related to Herman E. Calloway?
    The final proof was Bud's picture of his mother.

4. What did Bud realize about the dead girl's room?
    He realized that it was his mother's room.

5. What was so special about the picture that Miss Thomas gave Bud?
    Momma was smiling in the picture, and no matter which way you looked at the picture, she was still looking at you.

6. What was written on the stones, and why was it written on them?
    Before Herman Calloway went to Chicago to play a job when his daughter was four or five years old, he asked her what she wanted him to bring back for her. She asked for a rock. So, everywhere HEC went after that, he brought her a rock with the city and date written on it.

7. What did Miss Thomas ask Bud to be?
    She asked him to be patient with Mr. Calloway.

8. What did the guys in the band buy for Bud?
    They bought him a saxophone.

9. What was funny about Bud saying he would play his saxophone as well as the other band members played their instruments in about three weeks?
    He didn't realize that they had practiced years to learn to play that well, and here he was, going to do it in three weeks.

10. What did Bud put in Herman E. Calloway's room? Why?
    He left the flyers and rocks there because he thought they rightfully belonged to Herman E. Calloway.

11. Why did Bud put his mother's Miss B. Gotten Moon Park picture on the wall?
    "I'd been carrying Momma around for all this time and I'd finally put her somewhere where she wanted to be, back in her own bedroom, back amongst all her horses."

12. Why didn't Bud need his suitcase items anymore?
    He realized they had served their useful purpose, and he didn't need them now that he was home.

13. What did the squeaks and squawks of the saxophone sound like to Bud?
    They sounded like one door closing and another door opening.

MULTIPLE CHOICE STUDY/QUIZ QUESTIONS
Bud, Not Buddy

Chapter 1

1. What good news did Bud and Jerry get?
    - A. There would be a better-than-usual dinner that night.
    - B. They were going to be adopted.
    - C. They were going to foster homes.
    - D. They didn't have to do their usual chores.

2. According to Bud, did he have a better foster family assignment than Jerry did? Explain.
    - A. Yes, he was going to be with a boy close to his own age who would play with him.
    - B. Yes, he was going to be with three girls.
    - C. No, he was going to be with three girls who would fuss over him.
    - D. No, he was going to be with a boy close to his own age who would probably fight with him.

3. Why is six a tough age?
    - A. Grown-ups expect you to understand everything they say.
    - B. You start to lose teeth.
    - C. Grown-ups stop giving you little swats and start slugging you.
    - D. All of the above

4. What was printed on the blue flyer? Why was it special?
    - A. The flyer was an advertisement for Herman E. Calloway and the Dusky Devastators of the Depression and a picture of a man standing next to a giant fiddle. Bud thought the man might be his father.
    - B. The blue flyer had a picture of Bud's mother sitting on a horse at the Miss B. Gotten Moon Park. It was the only picture Bud had of his mother.
    - C. The blue flyer had a list of the contents of Bud's suitcase so he could check to see that nothing was missing.
    - D. The blue flyer was an advertisement for the mission where Bud sometimes ate. It was special because Bud needed the directions to the mission that were printed on it.

Bud, Not Buddy Multiple Choice Study/Quiz Questions page 2

<u>Chapter 2</u>
1. Identify Todd Amos.
    A. Todd Amos was Bud's best friend at the home.
    B. Todd Amos was Jerry's brother.
    C. Todd Amos was the nasty boy at Bud's foster home.
    D. Todd Amos was Bud's foster father.

2. What promise did Mr. and Mrs. Amos break?
    A. They said they wouldn't look in Bud's suitcase.
    B. They said Bud would have his own room.
    C. They said they would treat Bud as their own son.
    D. They said Bud wouldn't have to do any chores.

3. What warnings did Todd give Bud about the shed?
    A. It was full of snakes, bats, and ghosts.
    B. It was full of vampire bats, spiders and centipedes.
    C. A vampire lived in it.
    D. No one had come out of it alive.

Bud, Not Buddy Multiple Choice Study/Quiz Questions page 3

Chapter 3
1. What were the door knob guards in the shed?
    A. vampire bats
    B. lizard heads
    C. slippery locks
    D. fish heads

2. How did "Bugs" get his nickname?
    A. A cockroach crawled in his ear.
    B. He collected bugs.
    C. He liked to watch Bugs Bunny cartoons.
    D. He had bug-eyes.

3. What was the vampire bat?
    A. It was the thing that attacked Bud in the shed at the Amoses.
    B. It was Bud's favorite baseball bat.
    C. It was a hornets' nest
    D. It was a dusty, old pouch hanging in the shed.

4. Why did Bud get mad after he got out of the shed?
    A. He was mad because he had ripped his only pants.
    B. He was mad at himself for believing there was a vampire bat.
    C. He was mad at the Amoses for having a vampire bat in their shed.
    D. He was mad because he was scared and lonely and missed the home.

Chapter 4
1. Why was the first part of Bud's revenge plan to get the gun out of the way?
    A. He thought he might need it later, so he hid it where only he could find it.
    B. He knew it was valuable to the Amoses, and he wanted them to see it was missing so they would be upset and worry about that.
    C. It was in his way for the second part of the plan.
    D. He was afraid the Amoses would use it on him if things went wrong.

2. What was part two of Bud's revenge plan?
    A. He poured water on Todd's pajama bottoms while Todd slept, to induce him to wet the bed.
    B. He beat the stuffing out of Todd then ran away as fast as he could.
    C. He reported the Amoses to the authorities at the home so no other boys would have his same bad experience.
    D. He put the hornets' nest in Todd's bed.

Bud, Not Buddy Multiple Choice Study/Quiz Questions page 4

Chapter 5
1. Where did Bud go when he left the Amoses?
    A. Back to the home
    B. To find Bugs
    C. To find Jerry
    D. To the library

2. What did Bud's use of his blanket tell us about him?
    A. He was cold.
    B. He was smart, neat, and careful with his things.
    C. He was still really a baby.
    D. He had been injured escaping from the shed.

3. Why was Momma unhappy in the picture taken at the Miss B. Gotten Moon Park?
    A. Her father made her wear a filthy hat.
    B. The horse smelled bad.
    C. The photographer had been mean to her.
    D. All of the above

4. What did Momma tell Bud about his name?
    A. "Bud" was short for Budweiser, his father's favorite beer, which Bud had inadvertently taken a drink of when he was a toddler. It was a funny family incident that just stuck as a joke.
    B. Bud's real name was Beauregard, but folks called him "Bud" because it was shorter.
    C. Momma told Bud to "nevermind about your name; it's 'Bud' and that's it. Period."
    D. Momma chose "Bud" because he is like a flower blossom, full of love, waiting for the right warmth and care to open it up.

5. What did Momma tell Bud about doors?
    A. When one door closes, don't worry; another door opens.
    B. If you're scared of what's behind a door, just jam a chair under the knob and you'll be safe.
    C. Doors are just doors. Nothing to fear; nothing to anticipate.
    D. All of the above

Bud, Not Buddy Multiple Choice Study/Quiz Questions page 5

Chapter 6
1. Who was Clarence?
    A. Clarence was a boy at the mission.
    B. Clarence was a boy from the home who ate at the mission.
    C. Clarence was Bud's foster brother.
    D. Clarence was Bud.

2. What did Bud's pretend mother and daddy do that annoyed him?
    A. They smacked him on the back of the head.
    B. They ate like pigs.
    C. They kept all the good food for themselves and just gave him leftovers.
    D. All of the above

3. What did the sign hanging over the building at the mission say?
    A. "God Bless This Food"
    B. "There's no place like America today!"
    C. "Be Thankful For All That God Has Given You"
    D. "When One Door Closes, Another Door Opens"

Chapter 7
1. What happened to Miss Hill, the librarian?
    A. She got married and moved to Chicago.
    B. She got a job at a library in Chicago.
    C. She got married and moved to Grand Rapids.
    D. She enjoyed marital bliss in Flint.

2. What did the other librarian show Bud?
    A. She showed him Miss Hill's wedding invitation.
    B. She showed him that Civil War books have the best gory pictures.
    C. She showed him a secret room in the basement where he could sleep.
    D. She showed him how to use a mileage guide.

3. What did Bud know about the library door's closing?
    A. It meant that he was stuck in the library, but at least would be safe, for the night.
    B. It meant he would be out on the street with no shelter for the night.
    C. It was the kind of door Momma had told him about. Since it had closed, another door was about to open.
    D. He knew that someone had closed the door, so he was not alone.

Bud, Not Buddy Multiple Choice Study/Quiz Questions page 6

Chapter 8
1. Who attacked Bud under the tree at the library?
    A. Jerry
    B. Bugs
    C. Todd
    D. Clarence

2. What did Bugs and Bud decide to do?
    A. Go to Chicago
    B. Go to Grand Rapids
    C. Go to California
    D. Go to get further revenge on the Amoses

3. Why was "Hooperville" so hard to find?
    A. Bud couldn't find it in the mileage guide.
    B. It was a long way from Flint.
    C. It wasn't actually a town; it was just a make-shift place where homeless people gathered.
    D. People didn't want to be bothered to help Bud find it since he was just a kid.

4. How did Bugs rig the coin toss?
    A. He weighted one side of the coin.
    B. Both choices he gave Bud would mean that he, Bugs, would win.
    C. One of the boys at the home had given him a trick coin with both sides the same.
    D. He counted the number of times it flipped over before he caught it.

5. How did "Hooverville" get its name?
    A. Mr. Hoover, the inventor of the vacuum cleaner, was born there, and the town was named after him.
    B. No one really knew who lived there. It really should have been "Whoverville," but the original misspelling stuck.
    C. It was, in fact, named for a Mr. Hoover, but he had nothing to do with vacuum cleaners. He was a man who cared for the homeless.
    D. It was named for President Hoover, whom many people blamed for their unemployment.

6. What kind of a welcome did the boys get at Hooverville?
    A. They got a warm welcome.
    B. They got an indifferent welcome.
    C. People were downright unfriendly.
    D. It was a mixed welcome; some people were friendly, some weren't.

Bud, Not Buddy Multiple Choice Study/Quiz Questions page 7

7. What promise did the Hooverville woman make to Bud when she told him to leave his bags while he did the dishes? Did she keep the promise?
    A. She promised Bud she would pay him a nickel for doing the dishes, which she didn't do.
    B. She promised Bud his things would be safe; no one would bother them, which is what happened.
    C. She promised Bud she'd send a sweet little girl over to keep him company while he did the dishes, which she did.
    D. She promised Bud her husband would tell him about how to get on the train if he would wash the dishes, and her husband did.

8. Who was Deza Malone?
    A. Deza Malone was Bud's pretend sister at the mission.
    B. Deza Malone was the librarian.
    C. Deza Malone was a homeless orphan.
    D. Deza Malone befriended Bud while they did the dishes together.

9. What was Bud's reply when Deza said, ". . . But you have been staying in an orphanage"?
    A. He corrected her, saying he had been staying at a mission.
    B. He corrected her, saying he had been staying in a home.
    C. He corrected her, saying he had been staying with a foster family.
    D. He corrected her, saying he had been staying at a library.

10. Why did *Shenandoah* remind Deza of her mother and father?
    A. Her father had gone to the Shenandoah Valley to find work.
    B. Like the Indian couple, her parents were separated but still loved each other.
    C. Like the Shenandoah River, their love flowed freely.
    D. Deza's mother used to sing her that song when she was a toddler, before they lost their home and came onto bad times.

11. Why did Deza feel sorry for the people with the sick baby?
    A. They didn't have money for a doctor.
    B. They didn't have a home.
    C. They were too proud to let anyone help them.
    D. All of the above

12. Why did Bud start wondering if going to California was the right thing to do?
    A. He was scared of traveling on the trains.
    B. He liked Deza and had new friends here he didn't want to leave.
    C. He knew people in Flint who could help him, but knew no one in California.
    D. He thought it was more likely he could find his own family closer to Flint.

Bud, Not Buddy Multiple Choice Study/Quiz Questions page 8

13. What did the smell of Bud's blanket remind him of?
    A. It reminded him of the home.
    B. It reminded him of sleeping outdoors under the tree.
    C. It reminded him of Momma and when she used to read to him.
    D. It reminded him of a cocoon and how he was like a caterpillar waiting to become a butterfly.

14. Why did Bud try to fall asleep before Momma was done reading the story at night?
    A. He didn't like to be alone when she left after the story.
    B. He didn't like having to listen to her explanation of the story.
    C. He knew she was tired, so he didn't want her to have to read any more than was necessary.
    D. He always had pleasant dreams when he fell asleep before the story was over.

15. What caused Bud to jump straight up and bang his head on the top of the shack?
    A. A man shouting
    B. Deza shaking him
    C. Bugs yelling at him
    D. The train whistle

16. Why did Bud miss the train?
    A. He went back to find Deza and say goodbye.
    B. The police held him back.
    C. He got stuck in the stampede of men and boys.
    D. He stopped to pick up his blue flyer and stick it in his pocket.

17. Why did the police try to stop the people from getting on the train?
    A. The police were prejudiced; they didn't want any Black people on the train.
    B. The train was full.
    C. None of the people had tickets.
    D. The people were union members, and no union members were allowed on the train.

18. What happened to Hooverville?
    A. It was vacated after the train left.
    B. The police demolished it.
    C. A fire got out of control and burned it down.
    D. People were banished from it.

19. What did Bud realize about the names Caldwell and Calloway?
    A. They were very similar–similar enough that one could be an alias for the other.
    B. They were both common names.
    C. Calloway was an old spelling of Caldwell.
    D. All of the above

Bud, Not Buddy Multiple Choice Study/Quiz Questions page 9

Chapter 9
1. Where did Bud go after breakfast at the mission?
    A. He went to look for Deza.
    B. He went to the train station.
    C. He went to find his suitcase.
    D. He went to the library.

2. Why did Bud like Civil War books?
    A. He liked looking for his family's name in them.
    B. He liked history; it gave him a sense of roots that he didn't have with family.
    C. They smelled good and reminded him of when his mother read to him.
    D. They had the best gory pictures.

3. According to Bud, how are ideas like seeds?
    A. They start small and grow bigger than you ever thought they could.
    B. They don't take root unless you tend to them.
    C. They need a lot of weeding to keep the bad parts out.
    D. You have to dig a hole before they can really get started.

4. How did Bud get the idea that Herman E. Calloway might be his father?
    A. His mother told him.
    B. A kid teasing him bet him a nickel he didn't know who his father was. In desperation, Bud blurted out it was Herman E. Calloway before he really thought.
    C. The librarian suggested Bud should try to find Herman E. Calloway, so Bud assumed she must have known he was a relative.
    D. He could see the family resemblance in the picture.

5. Why did Bud decide to walk across the state of Michigan from Flint to Grand Rapids?
    A. He thought that if he would travel around the state he surely would find someone who was related to him.
    B. He wanted to find Miss Hill to see if she had any information that would help him.
    C. He knew he had to get out of Flint before the people from the home found him and sent him back there. He thought Grand Rapids was as good of a direction to go as any.
    D. He knew Herman E. Calloway was in Grand Rapids, and he wanted to find him.

Bud, Not Buddy Multiple Choice Study/Quiz Questions page 10

Chapter 10
1. What kid-like thing did Bud do when he came to the sign that marked the city limits of Flint?
    A. He spit on the sign.
    B. He threw a rock at the sign.
    C. He jumped back and forth over the imaginary line, in and out of Flint.
    D. He danced around it like a May Pole.

2. How did the man know that Bud was from Flint and was hungry?
    A. That he was from Flint was just a guess, but he heard Bud's stomach growl.
    B. He knew Bud's family.
    C. Bud told him.
    D. He guessed based on circumstantial evidence.

3. Why did Bud tell the man he had run away from Grand Rapids?
    A. He said that because it was true.
    B. He said that so the man would take him there.
    C. He said that just to tell him *something*; it didn't matter what.
    D. He said that thinking it would make the man leave him alone.

4. Why did Bud try to drive away the man's car?
    A. Bud just wanted to see if he could drive.
    B. Bud was afraid of the man because he thought he was a vampire.
    C. Bud decided to go to Grand Rapids on his own, and this was an opportunity to do that.
    D. The man made Bud angry; Bud's revenge was to take the car.

Bud, Not Buddy Multiple Choice Study/Quiz Questions page 11

Chapter 11
1. Why did Bud say that it's "terrible to have been brought up proper"?
    A. He can't not do the right thing.
    B. By having been brought up properly, he now knows the good things that are missing in his life.
    C. Because of his proper upbringing, he doesn't understand the way of life of the people who had not been brought up properly.
    D. People who had not been brought up properly thought less of him because of his manners and nice ways. They were mean to him and teased him.

2. Why did Bud insist on seeing the man's teeth?
    A. His mother used to tell him he could tell a man's character by his teeth.
    B. He wanted to make sure the man was not a vampire.
    C. Bud was afraid the man would bite him.
    D. Before he told the man that he had something dark stuck between his teeth, Bud wanted to make sure it was still there. Turned out that it was just an old filling.

3. Who was Lefty Lewis?
    A. A former boxing champion
    B. A gangster
    C. The man who befriended Bud
    D. All of the above

4. How did Bud know he was going to be safe?
    A. The moon was shining brightly down, just like it did when he was home with Momma.
    B. He just had a good feeling about Mr. Lewis.
    C. A policeman followed Lefty Lewis's car.
    D. He had never heard of a vampire that could drive a car and had never seen one that had such a good sense of humor.

5. Why did Bud sleep so well in the car and through that first night with Mr. Lewis?
    A. He could finally relax because he was safe.
    B. He was with someone who cared about him.
    C. He was finally on his way to meet Herman E. Calloway.
    D. All of the above

6. Why did Bud pretend to still be asleep even though he was awake?
    A. He didn't want to have to get out of bed; he was still tired.
    B. He wanted to eavesdrop some more.
    C. He was embarrassed.
    D. He was afraid.

Bud, Not Buddy Multiple Choice Study/Quiz Questions page 12

7. Who was Mrs. Sleet?
    A. Lefty Lewis "turned in" Bud to Mrs. Sleet from the orphanage.
    B. Mrs. Sleet was Lefty's friend.
    C. Mrs. Sleet was Lefty's daughter.
    D. Mrs. Sleet was, to Bud's surprise, the librarian!

8. What was Bud's reason for thinking it was okay to lie to an adult but not to a kid?
    A. Adults don't really care what you're saying as long as it accomplishes what they want in the end; kids really want to know.
    B. Adults are more used to lies than kids are.
    C. Adults actually expect kids to lie in certain circumstances; kids don't.
    D. It's more important what kids think of you than adults.

9. How was mealtime at the Sleets' house different from mealtime at the home?
    A. The Sleets had dessert.
    B. Everyone talked during meals at the Sleets' house.
    C. No one cared how you ate at the Sleets' house.
    D. All of the above

10. Who were "redcaps"?
    A. Redcaps were labor organizers.
    B. Redcaps were a baseball team.
    C. Redcaps were men who carried baggage at the train station.
    D. Redcaps were gangsters.

Bud, Not Buddy Multiple Choice Study/Quiz Questions page 13

Chapter 12
1. How was a telegram different from a regular letter?
    A. It wasn't actually printed.
    B. It was usually short because you had to pay by the letter.
    C. It was only used for emergencies.
    D. All of the above

2. Why did the policeman stop Lefty and search the car?
    A. He was looking for labor organizers.
    B. Lefty was speeding.
    C. He saw Lefty pick up Bud and wanted to make sure everything was all right.
    D. He had a report of gangsters in the area and was checking vehicles to try to catch them.

3. Why did Bud at first say he didn't think he needed to see what was in the box in Lefty's car?
    A. He thought it might be something really gruesome.
    B. He thought he would be better off not knowing.
    C. He didn't trust Lefty.
    D. All of the above

4. What was in the box in Lefty's car the day the policeman stopped him?
    A. blood
    B. flyers for a labor meeting
    C. a sandwich and a bottle of pop
    D. booze

5. Why would the workers go on a "sit down" strike instead of a regular strike?
    A. It was easier.
    B. Sit down strikes caused fewer legal problems.
    C. They still got paid that way.
    D. Sit down strikes kept management from bringing in new workers.

6. Why didn't Bud want Mr. Lewis to talk to Herman E. Calloway?
    A. He had sort-of lied to Mr. Lewis and had to figure a way out of it.
    B. He knew if he let the two talk, he'd be on the first transportation back to Flint.
    C. He had to see if Herman E. Calloway was his father first.
    D. All of the above

Bud, Not Buddy Multiple Choice Study/Quiz Questions page 14

7. Why did Lefty tell Bud to come see him if he decided to travel again?
    A. Lefty could get him onto the train for free.
    B. Lefty would want to help him if he could.
    C. Lefty had fun traveling with Bud and wanted to go, too, if Bud went.
    D. Lefty knew a lot of great places to go.

8. What immediate proof did Bud get that Herman E. Calloway was his father?
    A. Mr. Calloway welcomed him, "Son!"
    B. When Mr. Calloway turned around, he looked just like a grown-up Bud.
    C. Mr. Calloway was talking about Bud's mother.
    D. Mr. Calloway was talking using some of the same phrases Bud used.

9. What made Bud's "maple tree" shake in the wind?
    A. Herman E. Calloway was really old.
    B. Herman E. Calloway was mean and grumpy.
    C. Herman E. Calloway was crying.
    D. Herman E. Calloway was holding stones just like those Bud had gotten from his mother.

10. Why did Bud think he wasn't a "regular kid"?
    A. He was homeless.
    B. He was an orphan.
    C. He didn't cry.
    D. He was "brought up proper."

Bud, Not Buddy Multiple Choice Study/Quiz Questions page 15

Chapter 13
1. What was Bud's first impression of Herman E. Calloway?
   A. He'd be a swell dad.
   B. He seemed like he'd be hard to get along with.
   C. He smelled like stale smoke and booze.
   D. He was just an average guy but would do nicely as a dad.

2. Match the person with their instrument.
   ___ Doug "The Thug" Tennant   A. trombone
   ___ "Steady" Eddie Patrick   B. piano
   ___ Chug "Doo-Doo-Bug" Cross   C. drums
   ___ Roy "Dirty Deed" Breed   D. saxophone

3. Why did Bud slap his hand over his mouth?
   A. He was supposed to be quiet but he momentarily forgot.
   B. He swallowed an insect.
   C. He didn't want to say what he was about to say.
   D. He said something he shouldn't have said but realized it too late.

4. Why was Steady Eddie Bud's favorite?
   A. He looked the coolest.
   B. He stood up to Mr. Calloway.
   C. He was clearly on Bud's side and was looking out for him.
   D. He had the best sense of humor.

5. Identify *Sweet Pea*.
   A. Sweet Pea was the band's nickname for Herman E. Calloway.
   B. Sweet Pea was the band's code for "Mr. Calloway is coming."
   C. Sweet Pea was the name of the restaurant frequented by the band.
   D. Sweet Pea was Bud's nickname.

Bud, Not Buddy Multiple Choice Study/Quiz Questions page 16

Chapter 14
1. Who was Miss Thomas?
    A. She was Mr. Calloway's wife. She just used Thomas as a stage name.
    B. She was the band's vocalist who had a special relationship with Mr. Calloway.
    C. She was Herman E. Calloway's daughter.
    D. She was Lefty's daughter.

2. What hit Bud as hard as Snaggletooth MacNevin had smacked Herman E. Calloway?
    A. Mr. Calloway's fist hit him.
    B. The band's music did.
    C. Mr. Calloway's bad humor hit Bud hard.
    D. The realization that this was where he belonged hit Bud hard.

3. What did Bud decide when he realized that this was where he was supposed to be?
    A. He decided he would work hard and do everything he could to make everyone there love him.
    B. He decided that even thought it was where he was supposed to be, he didn't really like being there and would take the first opportunity to go back to Flint.
    C. He decided it would take a lot more than a grouchy, old, bald-headed guy with a tremendous belly to run him out.
    D. He decided Mr. Calloway wasn't really so bad after all.

4. Why did Bud cry?
    A. Herman E. Calloway wasn't his father; he was disappointed to have to keep looking for his relatives.
    B. He was happy and relieved to be home.
    C. He missed his mother and really wanted her advice.
    D. Miss Thomas reminded him so much of his mother; it was too much for him. He just broke down and cried.

Bud, Not Buddy Multiple Choice Study/Quiz Questions page 17

Chapter 15
1. What was Grand Calloway Station?
   A. It was the train station where Lefty worked.
   B. It was the nickname for the restaurant the band frequented.
   C. It was the nickname for Mr. Calloway's car.
   D. It was the nickname for Mr. Calloway's house.

2. What scared Bud the most when Miss Thomas showed him his room?
   A. The closet doors scared him.
   B. The pictures on the walls scared him.
   C. The fact it was closest to Mr. Calloway's room scared him.
   D. The fact that it belonged to a dead girl scared him.

3. What warning did Herman E. Calloway give Bud about snooping around the house?
   A. "There'll be no snoopin' around *my* house, young man! I'll put you on the first train back to wherever you come from if I catches you snoopin' in my things!"
   B. "Just remember: curiosity killed the cat."
   C. "I've got little secret bells all over everything and when something's stolen the bell goes off and only I can hear it, so watch your step."
   D. "Mess with any of my stuff, and I'll have Al Capone hot on your tail before you know it! Don't even think you can get away with anything here."

4. What was Bud's reaction to Herman E. Calloway's warning?
   A. He thought it was so ridiculous it was funny.
   B. He immediately wanted to steal something.
   C. He was scared to death.
   D. He wished he had never met Herman E. Calloway.

Bud, Not Buddy Multiple Choice Study/Quiz Questions page 18

Chapter 16
1. Why did Bud's eyes get all sting-y when he looked at his clothes in the morning?
    A. He was about to cry because that was how his mother had fixed his clothes for him.
    B. He wasn't awake yet and the clothes were in bright sunshine, making his eyes water.
    C. He was overwhelmed with embarrassment because someone had undressed him.
    D. All of the above

2. Why did Bud make so much noise when he came downstairs?
    A. He couldn't help it; he was a naturally loud kid.
    B. The new shoes they had left for him were clunking on the floor.
    C. He wanted to announce that he was arriving into the room.
    D. B and C

3. What did the band, Mr. Calloway, and Miss Thomas decide about Bud while he slept that first night?
    A. He should stay at Grand Calloway Station for a while.
    B. He was going to be a lot more trouble than they had anticipated.
    C. They would give him a few days and then send him back to Flint.
    D. All of the above

4. What did Steady Eddie give Bud? What might it symbolize?
    A. He gave Bud a new pair of shoes, symbolizing Bud's walking into a new life.
    B. He gave Bud a bath, symbolizing a baptism into a new life.
    C. He gave Bud a new sign for the door of his room, symbolizing the opening of a new door to a new life.
    D. He gave Bud an old saxophone case to replace his old suitcase, symbolizing Bud's new life.

5. What name did Bud get?
    A. They called him Sleepy LaBone.
    B. They called him Sweet Pea.
    C. They called him Suitcase.
    D. They called him Stones.

Chapter 17
1. Why was Herman E. Calloway doing a bad job of making Bud work like a dog?
    A. He didn't really want to make Bud work.
    B. He was just a terrible administrator.
    C. Bud was having fun in spite of the fact that it was supposed to be work.
    D. Mr. Calloway didn't really care.

Bud, Not Buddy Multiple Choice Study/Quiz Questions page 19

2. What did Bud say the band should be called?
    A. Miss Thomas and the Dusky Devastators of the Depression and a Mean Old Guy on the Giant Fiddle
    B. The Sleepy LaBone Band
    C. The Grand Calloway Band
    D. Three Cool Guys, A Pretty Lady, And A Mean Old Guy On The Giant Fiddle

Chapter 18

1. What were the band members' favorite things to do, according to Bud?
    A. Play music
    B. Tease each other
    C. Talk about Herman E. Calloway behind his back
    D. All of the above

2. What was the answer to Bud's question, "Why does he always keep one white guy in the band?"
    A. Mr. Calloway can't own property, so he put it in Deed's name.
    B. "For insurance purposes"
    C. ". . . a lot of these white folks wouldn't hire us if they knew we were a Negro band so Deed goes out and sets up everything."
    D. A & C

3. What unhappy news did Bud get when he was packing up at the Laughing Jackass?
    A. Mr. Calloway had a stroke.
    B. Miss Thomas was leaving the band.
    C. He had to ride home with Mr. Calloway.
    D. He had to leave Grand Calloway Station.

4. What finally convinced Herman E. Calloway that Bud might be his relative?
    A. The stones
    B. Bud's smile
    C. The way Bud talked
    D. Bud's music appreciation

Bud, Not Buddy Multiple Choice Study/Quiz Questions page 20

Chapter 19

1. What did Bud see that made his heart jump down into his stomach when he went upstairs to get the pictures?
    A. His suitcase was gone.
    B. His suitcase had been ransacked.
    C. Mr. Calloway was crying.
    D. Mr. Calloway's bells had gone off and the pictures were missing.

2. What was Herman E. Calloway trying to say to Bud when Bud touched him while they were in the dead girl's room?
    A. "Get out of my life!"
    B. "I love you."
    C. "I'm sorry."
    D. "I was right!"

3. What was the final proof that Bud was related to Herman E. Calloway?
    A. the stones
    B. his blood type
    C. Herman's confession
    D. the picture of his mother

4. What did Bud realize about the dead girl's room?
    A. It belonged to his mother.
    B. It made Herman E. Calloway happy.
    C. The closet connected to Mr. Calloway's room.
    D. It was kept better than any other room.

5. What was so special about the picture that Miss Thomas gave Bud?
    A. It was the first picture ever taken of his mother.
    B. Momma was smiling in it.
    C. Bud's mother had written him a note on the back.
    D. All of the above

6. What was written on the stones?
    A. Birth dates and birth places of Calloway relatives
    B. Books, chapters and verses from the Bible
    C. Dates and places Mr. Calloway's band had played
    D. Dates and places where Mr. Calloway and his daughter had met

Bud, Not Buddy Multiple Choice Study/Quiz Questions page 21

7. What did Miss Thomas ask Bud to be?
     A. Flexible to adapt to his new lifestyle
     B. Persistent in his music studies
     C. Patient with Mr. Calloway
     D. More helpful around the house

8. What did the guys in the band buy for Bud?
     A. A new suitcase
     B. A saxophone
     C. New clothes
     D. Dinner

9. What was funny about Bud saying he would play his saxophone as well as the other band members played their instruments in about three weeks?
     A. The band members had practiced for years to play well.
     B. It would take at least one month to play as well.
     C. Bud already knew how to play, he just needed the practice.
     D. Bud was a quick learner, so he know he would be able to place in three weeks.

10. What did Bud put in Herman E. Calloway's room?
     A. A picture of his mother
     B. Some flowers
     C. His old suitcase
     D. The rocks and flyers

11. Why did Bud put his mother's Miss B. Gotten Moon Park picture on the wall?
     A. He thought she'd want to be back in her own bedroom amongst all her horses.
     B. Mr. Calloway ordered him to do it.
     C. He didn't want to lose it in his travels with the band.
     D. Miss Thomas suggested it, and he thought it would be a good idea.

12. Why didn't Bud need his suitcase items anymore?
     A. He had new ones that the band had given him.
     B. They had served their useful purpose; he had found his home.
     C. He had grown up.
     D. They made him cry, so he wanted to get rid of them.

13. What did the squeaks and squawks of the saxophone sound like to Bud?
     A. Music
     B. Cacophony
     C. One door closing and another door opening
     D. The rhythm of his mother reading to him at night

ANSWER KEY - MULTIPLE CHOICE STUDY/QUIZ QUESTIONS
Bud, Not Buddy

Chapter 1
1. C   2. D   3. D   4. A

Chapter 2
1. C   2. A   3. B

Chapter 3
1. D   2. A   3. C   4. B

Chapter 4
1. D   2. A

Chapter 5
1. D   2. B   3. A   4. D   5. A

Chapter 6
1. D   2. A   3. B

Chapter 7
1. A   2. D   3. C

Chapter 8
1. B   2. C   3. C   4. B   5. D   6. A   7. B   8. D   9. B   10. B
11. D   12. D   13. C   14. B   15. A   16. D   17. C   18. B   19. A

Chapter 9
1. D   2. D   3. A   4. B   5. D

Chapter 10
1. C   2. D   3. B   4. B

Chapter 11
1. A   2. B   3. C   4. D   5. D   6. B   7. C   8. A   9. B   10. C

Chapter 12
1. B   2. A   3. B   4. B   5. D   6. D   7. B   8. D   9. A   10. C

Chapter 13
1. B   2. C, D, A, B   3. D   4. C   5. C

Bud, Not Buddy Multiple Choice Study/Quiz Key page 2

Chapter 14
1. B   2. D   3. C   4. B

Chapter 15
1. D   2. A   3. C   4. B

Chapter 16
1. A   2. C   3. A   4. D   5. A

Chapter 17
1. C   2. A

Chapter 18
1. D   2. D   3. C   4. A

Chapter 19
1. D   2. D   3. C   4. A   5. B   6. C   7. C   8. B   9. A   10. D
11. A   12. B   13. C

PREREADING VOCABULARY WORKSHEETS

VOCABULARY - *Bud, Not Buddy*

<u>Chapters 1-2</u>
Part I: Using Prior Knowledge and Contextual Clues

    Below are the sentences in which the vocabulary words appear in the text. Read the sentence. Use any clues you can find in the sentence combined with your prior knowledge, and write what you think the underlined words mean on the lines provided.

1. . . . you have both been accepted in new <u>temporary</u> care homes starting this afternoon.

_____

2. Now, now, boys, no need to look so <u>glum</u>. . . .We've been lucky enough to find two wonderful families who've opened their doors for you.

_____

3. . . . it's around six that grown folks stop giving you little swats and taps and jump clean up to giving you slugs that'll knock you right down and have you seeing stars in the middle of the day. The first <u>foster</u> home I was in taught me that real quick.

_____

4. Todd coughed out, "Oh, Mother. . ." He took two jumbo breaths. "I was only trying to help. . . ."–he was sounding like a horse that had been run too hard in the winter–"and look what it's gotten me." . . . With one quick snatch she had me from under the bed and out on the floor laying down next to Todd. "How dare you! This is how you choose to repay me? Not only have you struck him, you have <u>provoked</u> his <u>asthma</u>!"

_____

_____

5. You are a beastly little brute and I will not <u>tolerate</u> even one night with you under my roof.

_____

6. "Boy," Mrs. Amos said, "I am not the least bit surprised at your show of <u>ingratitude</u>. Lord knows I have been stung by my own people before. But take a good look at me because I am one person who is totally fed up with you and your <u>ilk</u>.

_____

_____

Bud, Not Buddy Vocabulary Chapters 1-2 Continued

7. I do not know if I shall ever be able to help another child in need. I do know I shall not allow <u>vermin</u> to attack my poor baby in his own house.

_____

8. We walked around to the back of the shed and he put a key in a padlock. . . . Mr. Amos <u>nudged</u> me and I took a baby step into the shed.

_____

Part II: Match the words to their dictionary definitions.

_____ 1. glum		A. illness causing difficulty breathing
_____ 2. temporary		B. unthankfulness
_____ 3. foster		C. started; induced
_____ 4. provoked		D. kind, group, sort, set
_____ 5. asthma		E. not permanent; just for a while
_____ 6. tolerate		F. sad
_____ 7. ingratitude		G. put up with; endure
_____ 8. ilk		H. lightly or gently pushed
_____ 9. vermin		I. low-life creatures like rats & mice
_____ 10. nudged		J. temporary care

Bud, Not Buddy Vocabulary Chapters 3-5

Part I: Using Prior Knowledge and Contextual Clues
  Below are the sentences in which the vocabulary words appear in the text. Read the sentence. Use any clues you can find in the sentence combined with your prior knowledge, and write what you think the underlined words mean on the lines provided.

1. I can't all the way blame Todd for giving me trouble, though. If I had a regular home with a mother and father I wouldn't be too happy about other kids living in my house, either. Being unhappy about it is one thing, but <u>torturing</u> the kids who are there even though they don't want to be is another.

_____

2. I dipped my finger in the water. It felt like the perfect <u>temperature</u>.

_____

3. I could tell right away that someone had been <u>fumbling</u> through my things. First off, Whenever I put the blanket in, I always fold it so that it stops all the other things from banging up against each other, but those doggone Amoses had just stuffed it in without paying no mind to what it was mashing up against.

_____

4. In the picture Momma was sitting on a real live little <u>midget</u> horse.

_____

5. But your grandfather <u>insisted</u>. To this day I cannot understand why, but he <u>insisted, insisted</u>.

_____

6. I'd have to wake up real early if I wanted to get to the <u>mission</u> in time for breakfast, if you were one minute late they wouldn't let you in for food.

_____

Bud, Not Buddy Vocabulary Chapters 3-5 Continued

II. Determining the Meaning - Match the words to their dictionary definitions.

_____ 1. torturing   A. repeatedly demanded
_____ 2. temperature   B. small in size
_____ 3. fumbling   C. charitable, usually religious, place of help for the needy
_____ 4. midget   D. mistreating, tormenting, abusing
_____ 5. insisted   E. hotness or coolness
_____ 6. mission   F. clumsily handling things

Bud, Not Buddy Vocabulary Chapters 6-7

Part I: Using Prior Knowledge and Contextual Clues
Below are the sentences in which the vocabulary words appear in the text. Read the sentence. Use any clues you can find in the sentence combined with your prior knowledge, and write what you think the underlined words mean on the lines provided.

1. PLEASE EAT AS QUICKLY AND QUIETLY AS POSSIBLE . . . BE CONSIDERATE AND PATIENT – CLEAN UP AFTER YOURSELF–YOUR NEIGHBORS WILL BE EATING AFTER YOU

_____

_____

2. Then I could sniff the paper, that soft, powdery, drowsy smell that comes off the pages in little puffs when you're reading something or looking at some pictures, a kind of hypnotizing smell.

_____

3. Really, it's not bd news. Unless you had matrimonial plans concerning Miss Hill. . . . I don't think her new husband would appreciate the competition.

_____

_____

4. "You mean she got married, ma'am?" The librarian said, "Oh, yes, and I must tell you she was radiating happiness."

_____

Part II: Determining the Meaning - Match the words to their dictionary definitions.

_____ 1. considerate   A. able to wait
_____ 2. patient   B. shining, beaming, giving off rays
_____ 3. hypnotizing   C. relating to marriage
_____ 4. matrimonial   D. thinking of what will benefit others
_____ 5. appreciate   E. having the effect of putting one in a trance or asleep
_____ 6. radiating   F. being glad or thankful for something;
                                 noting something's worth

Bud, Not Buddy Vocabulary Chapter 8

Part I: Using Prior Knowledge and Contextual Clues

    Below are the sentences in which the vocabulary words appear in the text. Read the sentence. Use any clues you can find in the sentence combined with your prior knowledge, and write what you think the underlined words mean on the lines provided.

1. "Did the guy cry after you whupped him?" "Well, kind of, he looked real scared, then told his momma to keep me away from him. They even said I was a hoodlum."

   _____

2. Me, Bugs, a little white boy and a little girl loaded a whole mess of dirty tin cans and spoons and a couple of real plates and forks into a big wooden box and lugged them down to Thread Crick.

   _____

3. A man screamed, "Get up . . ." Bugs and the other boys came and stood next to me. Bugs said, "Is it a raid?" Someone said, "No, they're trying to sneak out before we get up."

   _____

4. It seemed like we stood looking at the cops and them looking at us for a whole hour. Our side was getting bigger and bigger and the other cops started looking nervous. The one who was doing all the talking saw them fidgeting and said, "Hold steady, men."

   _____

5. But it was like a miracle, the flyer flipped over three times and landed right in my hand.

   _____

Part II: Determining the Meaning - Match the words to their dictionary definitions.

      _____ 1. hoodlum   A. small-time criminal
      _____ 2. lugged   B. nervously moving about or twitching
      _____ 3. raid   C. an act of God
      _____ 4. fidgeting   D. carried
      _____ 5. miracle   E. attack or invasion, sometimes to uncover something illegal

Bud, Not Buddy Vocabulary Chapters 9-10
Part I: Using Prior Knowledge and Contextual Clues
Below are the sentences in which the vocabulary words appear in the text. Read the sentence. Use any clues you can find in the sentence combined with your prior knowledge, and write what you think the underlined words mean on the lines provided.

1. You know, after I went home last night I finally <u>recognized</u> you. Didn't you and your mother used to come in here a long time ago?

   _____

2. I figured it would be easiest to do the night part first so I <u>decided</u> to stick around the library until it got dark, then head for Grand Rapids.

   _____

3. One second I was opening the first page of the book . . . and the next second the librarian was standing over me saying, "I am very impressed, you really <u>devoured</u> that book, didn't you?"

   _____

4. I was carefuller talking to him this time so he couldn't track where I was. I turned my head and talked sideways out of my mouth like one of those <u>ventriloquists</u>.

   _____

5. "Could you put them down and I'll eat them and you can keep driving, sir?" He laughed again. "Thanks for your <u>concern</u>, but I've got a little time to spare."

   _____

6. He handed me the bottle of red pop. H must've had it sitting in ice in the car, it was cold and sweet and <u>delicious</u>.

   _____

Part II: Determining the Meaning - Match the words to their dictionary definitions.

_____ 1. recognized   A. worry or care
_____ 2. decided   B. made a choice
_____ 3. devoured   C. tastes good
_____ 4. ventriloquist   D. identified
_____ 5. concern   E. ate completely or hungrily
_____ 6. delicious   F. performer who can make his voice appear to come from somewhere other than himself

Bud, Not Buddy Vocabulary Chapter 11

Part I: Using Prior Knowledge and Contextual Clues

Below are the sentences in which the vocabulary words appear in the text. Read the sentence. Use any clues you can find in the sentence combined with your prior knowledge, and write what you think the underlined words mean on the lines provided.

1. Now you stop being so judgmental, Herman's got a <u>reputation</u> for being no-nonsense, not mean.

   _____

2. As soon as they were a little bit down the hall I could hear her start in on <u>scolding</u> her father again. "I just can't believe it. You know, Momma was right about you. . . ." All I could hear next was him mumbling some answer, then her slapping his arm again.

   _____

3. The new clothes were just a little bit too big, but they were long pants and not <u>knickers</u> so I didn't care, I rolled cuffs into the pants and sleeves and they fit pretty doggone good.

   _____

4. . . . she used to be such a bad cook that her fried chicken was known to have turned a chicken hawk into a <u>vegetarian</u>.

   _____

Part II: Determining the Meaning - Match the words to their correct definitions.

_____ 1. reputation   A. lecturing; reprimanding
_____ 2. scolding   B. short pants
_____ 3. knickers   C. a person's character as observed by others
_____ 4. vegetarian   D. one who does not eat meat

Bud, Not Buddy Vocabulary Chapters 12-19

Part I: Using Prior Knowledge and Contextual Clues
     Below are the sentences in which the vocabulary words appear in the text. Read the sentence. Use any clues you can find in the sentence combined with your prior knowledge, and write what you think the underlined words mean on the lines provided.

1. Whoever heard of someone's momma naming him Lefty? That name had <u>alias</u> written all over it. Lefty sounds like a real good name for a stick-up man. (Chapter 12)

_____

2. Herman E. Calloway said, "I am truly sorry to hear that, but it's <u>obvious</u> that you are a disturbed young man and you don't have a clue who your father is. You just tell us who's looking after you now, and we'll get you sent back to wherever it is you belong." (Chapter 13)

_____

3. He talked out of the side of his mouth and kept his eyes kind of blinked halfway down, <u>especially</u> when Miss Tyla would come to our table to see if we were all right. . . . (Chapter 14)

_____

4. The way he was so worried about me staling stuff from him before he even knew if I was honest or not made me wonder if someone who was so <u>suspicious</u> could ever be <u>kin</u> to me. (Chapter 15)

_____

_____

5. . . . if you're going to be traveling with us it just wouldn't look too <u>copacetic</u> for you to be carrying that ratty old bag. (Chapter 16)

_____

6. Mr. Jimmy said, "Now hold on, Grace, I'm just trying to ask the questions I know Herman'd ask if he could. Ain't a thing wrong with being certain before we jump to any <u>conclusions</u>. (Chapter 19)

_____

Bud, Not Buddy Vocabulary Chapters 12-19 Continued

7. "We've been hoping for eleven years that she'd send word or come home, and she finally has. Looks to me like she sent us the best word we've had in years." Miss Thomas smiled at me and I know she was trying to say I was the word that my momma had sent to them. She said, "Wait here for one second, <u>precious</u>. I've got to go to my room for something." (Chapter 19)

___

8. That <u>ornery</u> old man upstairs is very, very hurt right now and I just can't say where he's going to land after this news gets through blowing him around. (Chapter 19)

___

9. "I told the fellas how hard you've been hitting that recorded and how proud I was of you, so we put a couple of nickels together"–he acted like he was yelling into the other room–"and Lord knows on the peanuts we get it was a real <u>sacrifice</u>." (Chapter 19)

___

Part II: Determining the Meaning - Match the words to their dictionary definitions.

_____ 1. alias   A. relatives
_____ 2. obvious   B. particularly
_____ 3. especially   C. proper
_____ 4. suspicious   D. hardship
_____ 5. kin   E. valuable
_____ 6. copacetic   F. easy to see
_____ 7. conclusions   G. wary; not trusting
_____ 8. precious   H. a made-up name usually assumed to hide one's true identity
_____ 9. ornery   I. results, decisions, deductions
_____10. sacrifice   J. causing trouble

ANSWER KEY - VOCABULARY
Bud, Not Buddy

Chapters 1-2	Chapters 3-5	Chapters 6-7	Chapter 8
1. F	1. D	1. D	1. A
2. E	2. E	2. A	2. D
3. J	3. F	3. E	3. E
4. C	4. B	4. C	4. B
5. A	5. A	5. F	5. C
6. G	6. C	6. B	
7. B			
8. D			
9. I			
10. H			

Chapters 9-10	Chapter 11	Chapters 12-19
1. D	1. C	1. H
2. B	2. A	2. F
3. E	3. B	3. B
4. F	4. D	4. G
5. A		5. A
6. C		6. C
		7. F
		8. E
		9. J
		10. D

DAILY LESSONS

LESSON ONE

Objectives
1. To introduce *Bud, Not Buddy* unit.
2. To distribute books and other related materials (study guides, reading assignments, etc.).
3. To preview the study questions for chapters 1-2
4. To familiarize students with the vocabulary for chapters 1-2
5. To explain the Group Work Project for this unit

Activity #1
 Distribute the materials students will use in this unit. Explain in detail how students are to use these materials.

Study Guides Students should read the study guide questions for each reading assignment prior to beginning the reading assignment to get a feeling for what events and ideas are important in the section they are about to read. After reading the section, students will (as a class or individually) answer the questions to review the important events and ideas from that section of the book. Students should keep the study guides as study materials for the unit test.

Vocabulary Prior to reading a reading assignment, students will do vocabulary work related to the section of the book they are about to read. Following the completion of the reading of the book, there will be a vocabulary review of all the words used in the vocabulary assignments. Students should keep their vocabulary work as study materials for the unit test.

Reading Assignment Sheet You (the teachers) need to fill in the reading assignment sheet to let students know by when their reading has to be completed. You can either write the assignment sheet up on a side blackboard or bulletin board and leave it there for students to see each day, or you can "ditto" copies for each student to have. In either case, you should advise students to become very familiar with the reading assignments so they know what is expected of them.

Extra Activities Center The Unit Resource Materials portion of this unit contains suggestions for an extra library of related books and articles in your classroom as well as crossword and word search puzzles. Make an extra activities center in your room where you will keep these materials for students to use. (Bring the books and articles in from the library and keep several copies of the puzzles on hand.) Explain to students that these materials are available for students to use when they finish reading assignments or other class work early.

<u>Nonfiction Assignment Sheet</u> Explain to students that they each are to read at least one non-fiction piece from the in-class library at some time during the unit. Students will fill out a nonfiction assignment sheet after completing the reading to help you (the teacher) evaluate their reading experiences and to help the students think about and evaluate their own reading experiences. Students may use the information they read for the introductory research project to fulfill their nonfiction reading assignment for this unit.

<u>Books</u> Each school has its own rules and regulations regarding student use of school books. Advise students of the procedures that are normal for your school.

Activity #3

There are many symbols, ideas and things that thread throughout this book. Rather than waiting until the end of the book and then digging back through it to make some sense of them, this unit proposes a group work project throughout the unit. Divide your students into groups, assigning one topic to each group. Time is allotted every few days for the groups to meet to collect data from the chapters they have read and to discuss that data. After the reading is completed, students will have a class period to put their notes together and prepare presentations which will incorporate a class discussion of each topic presented. The group assignment description follows this page. We suggest you make copies of the assignments for your students to have and follow.

> Note: This project has been set up with several objectives in mind. The most obvious objective is to get the information pulled out of the book and compiled so it is easier to look at and discuss. However, by doing this project in the way it is outlined, students also do critical reading, critical thinking, cooperative learning to share ideas and listen to others' ideas, note-taking, data gathering and analysis, presentation preparation, public speaking/oral presentations, math (to calculate page assignments), writing, and evaluating. Other skills are also incorporated depending on the category of the group (for example, map reading skills for the group dealing with places and maps).

Tell each student which group category he or she is assigned.

Activity #4

Use the remainder of this class time to show students how to preview the study questions for chapters 1-2, a process they will repeat for each chapter assignment. Also, show students how to do the vocabulary pre-reading worksheets using the one for chapters 1-2 as an example. Some teachers have done these vocabulary worksheets orally with students as a whole-class activity by making a transparency for the overhead projector so all students can see the worksheet. Some teachers have also given students their own copies of the worksheets to complete as the class does the one on the overhead projector so that students will have correct answers to study from. Of course, the worksheets may also be completed individually and independently by students if you choose not to use them as a whole-class activity. If time permits, begin reading chapters 1-2 in class. Any of the work discussed in this Activity #4 that is not completed by the end of the class period should be assigned as homework.

NONFICTION ASSIGNMENT SHEET
(To be completed after reading the required nonfiction article)

Name _____ Date _____

Title of Nonfiction Read _____

Written By _____ Publication Date _____

I. Factual Summary: Write a short summary of the piece you read.

II. Vocabulary
    1. With which vocabulary words in the piece did you encounter some degree of difficulty?

    2. How did you resolve your lack of understanding with these words?

III. Interpretation: What was the main point the author wanted you to get from reading his work?

IV. Criticism
    1. With which points of the piece did you agree or find easy to accept? Why?

    2. With which points of the piece did you disagree or find difficult to believe? Why?

V. Personal Response: What do you think about this piece? OR How does this piece influence your ideas?

GROUP WORK PROJECT ASSIGNMENT
Bud, Not Buddy

Introduction

Bud, Not Buddy is a fun story to read, but it also has many literary devices used in it not only to make it enjoyable to read but which give the book depth in meaning and a richness beyond just the surface story. For *each* of us to find *all* of these things as we read the story would be a mind-boggling undertaking, as would going back after the reading to find them all. So, to enhance our enjoyment and understanding of the book as we read it (and to keep us from having to do a TON of work digging around in it afterwards), you will be assigned specific things to look for as you read. We have five categories of things to look for, so we'll break into five groups with the members of each group looking for things related to their category.

The Categories

The categories of things we'll be looking for are as follows:

Group 1:   Names & Places
Group 2:   Rules and Things
Group 3:   Doors
Group 4:   The Suitcases
Group 5:   The Writing

There are, of course, many other things in the book we'll discuss both as we go along and afterwards, but these things are scattered throughout the book. Keeping track of them as we go along will help you better understand the whole book in the end.

Your Assignment

Each group has the same basic tasks which are as follows:

-- Each student in the group must keep his/her own list of examples where things related to the category appear in the book. The list should give the chapter and page number where the thing occurs, the direct quote from the book where it occurs, and your thoughts/group's comments about that instance.

-- Each time your group is given time to meet in class, you should look back through the chapters covered since your last group meeting, find the places where something related to your category occurs, and update your lists.

   Take a few minutes at the beginning of your group time to see how many pages need to be covered in that group session. Divide the number of pages by the number of students in your group and assign each student in the group certain pages to search. For example, if chapters 1-2 have 20 pages and there are 5 students in your group, each student would only have to carefully re-read 4 pages. One student would get pages 1-4, another would do 5-8, another 9-12, and so on.

   After each of you has carefully re-read your pages, you should get back together as a group to share what you have found and update your lists so all of you have written on your lists everything everyone has found.

Bud, Not Buddy Group Work Project Assignment page 2

As you update your lists by telling each other what you have found, take a few extra minutes to talk about the significance, meaning, or importance of each thing you found. Jot down the comments made onto your lists.

-- After the class has finished reading the book, you will be given one class period to meet again as a group to complete your lists, compile your thoughts, and create a presentation about your category for the class.

Your class presentation should include:
One copy of your compiled list for each student in the class
An oral presentation by one or more group members giving a brief review of the data collected on the list
An oral presentation by one or more group members giving a summary of what your group concluded about the topic of its category (If you were the teacher giving a short lecture about this aspect of the book, what would you say? *That* should be in this part of the presentation.)
A discussion element in which you give your classmates time to ask questions and voice their opinions relating to your category
Audio/visual aids when they help to clarify your point(s) You should use visual aids *if they help to clarify your point(s)*. They are not required for every group, but if you can think of something that would *help* your classmates get what you are saying, please use it.

-- Each group participant must complete and submit a group member evaluation form.

Specific Category Instructions
What exactly are you looking for? Read the notes under your category for additional details.

Group 1: Names & Places
You are looking for names of people and places in the book, specifically, names of characters in the book and the places they go. Your list will include the name of the person or place, and your comment(s) about why the author chose that name (how that name is appropriate considering the person or place it is naming). You do not have to give the chapter and page number for every instance where the name "Bud" or "Herman E. Calloway" or "Momma" or "Flint" is used, but you should note pages or chapters which contain key information about that person or place (and note why it is important information). You *do* need to give specific chapter and page numbers for minor, yet important, characters like Deza Malone who only show up in the book for a short time. Use some common sense to determine what might be needed for each name. Try to decide as a group what should be done. If you have questions, of course, ask me.
You do not have to do historical people Bud often refers to in the book: Al Capone, President Hoover, etc. We will work with these names separately. *You only need to do names of characters who are a part of the story.*

Bud, Not Buddy Group Work Project Assignment page 3

Group 2: Rules & Things
As you read the book, you'll see that Bud has developed his own "Rules & Things" regarding certain life situations. Bud also has been "brought up proper" by his mother and has a definite code of ethics not only that she has instilled in him, but also ethics he has figured out on his own. *Your assignment is to track down the rules and things by which Bud lives.*

These will obviously include the "Rules & Things" actually stated in the book, but will also include more subtle rules not necessarily directly stated. It may be something he says he's figured out about how to deal with a particular thing. It may be something he shows in the way he acts or things he says. It may be something someone in the book observes about him. It's your job to dig Bud's rules for living out of the book.

Group 3: Doors
Doors, doors, doors are everywhere in this book, both literally and figuratively. Momma told Bud not to worry because when one door shuts another door opens. It's your assignment to find all the places where doors are mentioned and figure out why they're mentioned and what they might symbolically mean.

Group 4: The Suitcases
Your assignment includes following Bud's suitcases and their contents through the book and figuring out their significance. Bud has one suitcase through most of the book but acquires a "new" one near the end. When do the suitcases show up? Where are the references to each of the contents? What is happening in the story when the suitcases or their contents appear, and how could each instance be symbolically significant?

Group 5: The Writing
Bud, Not Buddy is just plain fun to read. It's your job to look at the *writing* of the book to see how the author makes this book work. Part of the author's craft was choosing to write it as a first person narrative, so we see the story and the world through Buddy. He's a charming, smart, and often unintentionally funny guy. <u>Look particularly at descriptions, humor, and figures of speech/slang/idioms.</u> What descriptive passages in the book are humorous and why? What is it about the descriptions that not only entertains us but gives us a very clear picture of what Bud means? What kinds of humor are in the book? What kinds of things are "funny," either intentionally or unintentionally? What is the effect? What phrases in the book stand out? Two that immediately come to my mind are "busted slob" with a girl (meaning "kissed" a girl) and "the coppers would plug me," meaning "the police would shoot me." Look for slang, idioms, figures of speech, phrases, words that add to the book's character and meaning.

<u>Conclusion</u>
Part of the reason for doing this project is to help you become a more critical reader; to notice things of importance as you read. You should also gain some experience in taking notes, in figuring out what is important enough to write down and in creating a format for your notes that will help you when you look back at them to analyze them. Naturally, we want to look more closely at *Bud, Not Buddy*, but there are lots of skills you can practice and sharpen during this unit which you should apply to other books you read and projects you do in the future.

GROUP MEMBER EVALUATION FORM
Bud, Not Buddy

Part of the challenge in doing group work is to evaluate each group member fairly on the work he or she does. Often students complain that they got "dumped on" by the other group members or that some group members did little or nothing to contribute. As I observe you working in class, I can see who is working and contributing and who isn't. The purpose of this form is two-fold. First, it is your opportunity to voice your point of view about who accomplished what in your group. Secondly, it is an exercise in evaluating and assessing your own and another person's (or other people's) work. An employer might ask you, "So, what have you done?" and you'll need to evaluate what you have done. Or, you might be the employer who needs to determine who gets a raise and who does not, who gets a promotion and who does not, or as a supervisor, you may need to fill out evaluations for personnel files of those you supervise. **Be fair, be honest, be complete.**

Group Name: _____ Date: _____

Evaluation Completed By: _____

1. How did the group work as a whole? How well did your group accomplish the assignment? Note any problems you had. Note anything you feel you did exceptionally well as a group.

2. Your Name _____
   How would you rate your work? (Check one box.)
   ( )A+   ( )A   ( )A/B   ( )B   ( )B/C   ( )C   ( )C/D   ( )D   ( )D/E   ( )E
   What, exactly, did you do? Be specific.

3. Group Member Name _____
   How would you rate this person's work? (Check one box.)

   ( )A+   ( )A   ( )A/B   ( )B   ( )B/C   ( )C   ( )C/D   ( )D   ( )D/E   ( )E
   What, exactly, did this person do? Be specific.

Bud, Not Buddy Group Member Evaluation Form page 2

4. Group Member Name _____
   How would you rate this person's work? (Check one box.)

   ( )A+   ( )A   ( )A/B   ( )B   ( )B/C   ( )C   ( )C/D   ( )D   ( )D/E   ( )E
   What, exactly, did this person do? Be specific.

5. Group Member Name _____
   How would you rate this person's work? (Check one box.)

   ( )A+   ( )A   ( )A/B   ( )B   ( )B/C   ( )C   ( )C/D   ( )D   ( )D/E   ( )E
   What, exactly, did this person do? Be specific.

6. Group Member #1 Name _____
   How would you rate this person's work? (Check one box.)

   ( )A+   ( )A   ( )A/B   ( )B   ( )B/C   ( )C   ( )C/D   ( )D   ( )D/E   ( )E
   What, exactly, did this person do? Be specific.

7. Group Member Name _____
   How would you rate this person's work? (Check one box.)

   ( )A+   ( )A   ( )A/B   ( )B   ( )B/C   ( )C   ( )C/D   ( )D   ( )D/E   ( )E
   What, exactly, did this person do? Be specific.

LESSON TWO

Objectives
1. To review the main ideas and events from chapters 1-2
2. To preview and read chapters 3-5
3. To give students time to begin working on their group projects

Activity #1
Give students a few minutes to formulate answers for the study guide questions for chapters 1-2, and then discuss the answers to the questions in detail. Write the answers on the board or overhead transparency so students can have the correct answers for study purposes.

Note: It is a good practice in public speaking and leadership skills for individual students to take charge of leading the discussions of the study questions. Perhaps a different student could go to the front of the class and lead the discussion each day that the study questions are discussed during this unit. Of course, the teacher should guide the discussion when appropriate and be sure to fill in any gaps the students leave.

Activity #2
Break students into their groups and give them time to work on their assignments for chapters 1-2. Depending on the length of your class period, you might give them a certain number of minutes to work or give them the remainder of the class period. If you give them a certain number of minutes, proceed with Activity #3 after their time is up. If you give them the rest of the class time to do Activity #2, tell them to proceed with previewing and reading chapters 3-5 when they finish with their group work.

Activity #3
Tell students to preview the study questions, do the pre-reading vocabulary worksheet and do the reading for chapters 3-5. If this is not completed in class, students should finish it for homework.

LESSON THREE

Objectives
    1. To review the main ideas and events of chapters 3-5
    2. To preview and read chapters 6-7

Activity #1
    Give students a few minutes to formulate answers for the study guide questions for chapters 3-5, and then discuss the answers to the questions in detail. Write the answers on the board or overhead transparency so students can have the correct answers for study purposes. (Remember the multiple choice format is always available any time you choose to give a quiz instead of doing the review this way.)

Activity #2
    Tell students that prior to the next class meeting, they should have done the pre-reading vocabulary, and reading work for chapters 6-7.

LESSON FOUR

Objectives
    1. To review the main ideas and events from chapters 6-7
    2. To preview and read chapter 8
    3. To give students time to on their group projects

Activity #1
    Give students a few minutes to formulate answers for the study guide questions for chapters 6-7, and then discuss the answers to the questions in detail. Write the answers on the board or overhead transparency so students can have the correct answers for study purposes.

Activity #2
    Break students into their groups and give them time to work on their assignments for chapters 3-7. Depending on the length of your class period, you might give them a certain number of minutes to work or give them the remainder of the class period. If you give them a certain number of minutes, proceed with Activity #3 after their time is up. If you give them the rest of the class time to do Activity #2, tell them to proceed with previewing and reading chapter 8 when they finish with their group work.

Activity #3
    Tell students to preview the study questions, do the pre-reading vocabulary worksheet and do the reading for chapter 8. If this is not completed in class, students should finish it for homework.

LESSON FIVE

Objectives
    1. To review the main ideas and events from chapter 8
    2. To give students the opportunity to practice writing their own opinions
    3. To get students to think about how a statement can mean different things depending on who reads or hears it
    4. To assign the pre-reading and reading work for chapters 9-10

Activity #1
    Give students a few minutes to formulate answers for the study guide questions for chapter 8, and then discuss the answers to the questions in detail. Write the answers on the board or overhead transparency so students can have the correct answers for study purposes.

Activity #2
    Tell students that prior to your next class meeting they should have completed the pre-reading and reading work for chapters 9-10. If they finish the writing assignment early, they may begin this reading assignment.

Activity #3
    Distribute Writing Assignment #1. Discuss the directions in detail and give students ample time to complete the assignment.

WRITING ASSIGNMENT #1 - *Bud, Not Buddy*

From Bud, Not Buddy, Chapter 6

The main thing people were talking about was the great big sign that was hanging over the building.

It showed a gigantic picture of a family of four rich white people sitting in a car driving somewhere. You could tell it was a family 'cause they all looked exactly alike. The only difference amongst them was that the daddy had a big head and a hat and the momma had the same head with a woman's hat and the girl had two big yellow pigtails coming out from above her ears. They all had big shiny teeth and big shiny eyes and big shiny cheeks and big shiny smiles. Shucks, you'd need to squint your eyes if that shiny family drove anywhere near you.

You could tell they were rich 'cause the car looked like it had room for eight or nine more people in it and 'cause they had movie star clothes on. The woman was wearing a coat with a hunk of fur around the neck and the man was wearing a suit and a tie and the kids looked like they were wearing ten-dollar-apiece jackets.

Writ about their car in fancy letters it said, THERE'S NO PLACE LIKE AMERICA TODAY!

My pretend daddy read it and said, "Uh-uh-uh, well, you got to give them credit, you wouldn't expect that they'd have the nerve to come down here and tell the truth."

PROMPT

When you say or write something to someone, you have to choose your words carefully and consider the person to whom you are speaking or writing. The same simple words can convey one meaning to one person and mean something quite different to someone else. Consider the passage written above. ***Your assignment is to write three paragraphs, one answering each of these questions***: What would THERE'S NO PLACE LIKE AMERICA TODAY! mean to a middle or upper class white person reading the sign driving by the mission? What did it mean to the poor, black man eating at the mission? What would that sign mean to you today if you were to see it?

PREWRITING

Divide a sheet of paper into three equal sections. Pretend you're a middle or upper class white person driving by the mission, and you see the sign. In the first section of your page, jot down some words and phrases that express your reaction. In the second section of your page, jot down some words and phrases that would express your reaction if you were poor and black and eating at the mission. Finally, in the third box, jot down some words and phrases that tell how you would feel today if you would see that sign.

DRAFTING

Consider the words and phrases in the first section of your page. If you could sum up the thoughts there into one sentence, what would it say? Write it down. Fill in the rest of your paragraph explaining your first sentence. Why would you interpret the sign that way, why would you feel that way about what the sign said? Do the same for each of your other two paragraphs.

Bud, Not Buddy Writing Assignment #1 page 2

PROOFREADING
When you finish the rough draft of your composition, ask a student who sits near you to read it. After reading your rough draft, he/she should tell you what he/she liked best about your work, which parts were difficult to understand, and ways in which your work could be improved. Reread your paper considering your critic's comments, and make the corrections you think are necessary.

FINAL DRAFT
Do a final proofreading of your paper double-checking your grammar, spelling, organization, and the clarity of your ideas. Write a good, final copy of your writing assignment to submit for a grade.

LESSON SIX

Objectives
    1. To review the main ideas and events of chapters 9-10
    2. To give the groups time to work on their topics for chapters 8-10
    3. To preview and read chapter 11

Activity #1

    Give students a few minutes to formulate answers for the study guide questions for chapters 9-10, and then discuss the answers to the questions in detail. Write the answers on the board or overhead transparency so students can have the correct answers for study purposes. (Remember the multiple choice format is always available any time you choose to give a quiz instead of doing the review this way.)

Activity #2

    Break students into their groups and give them time to work on their assignments for chapters 8-10. Depending on the length of your class period, you might give them a certain number of minutes to work or give them the remainder of the class period. If you give them a certain number of minutes, proceed with Activity #3 after their time is up. If you give them the rest of the class time to do Activity #2, tell them to proceed with previewing and reading chapter 11 when they finish with their group work.

Activity #3

    Tell students that prior to the next class meeting, they should have done the pre-reading vocabulary, and reading work for chapter 11. You could do parts of this as class activity or let students do the whole thing independently, whichever suits your class and your teaching style.

LESSON SEVEN

Objectives
1. To review the main ideas and events from chapter 11
2. To explore many of the people, events, and things Bud refers to in the book
3. To give students the opportunity to practice research skills, note-taking, and report writing
4. To give the teacher the opportunity to evaluate students' writing skills
5. To do the pre-reading and reading work for chapters 12-13

Activity #1
Distribute Writing Assignment #2. Discuss the directions in detail. Give students ample time to complete the assignment. This is not intended to be a long and involved research assignment; rather, an exercise in finding information, taking notes, going from notes to written report, and actually gaining a working knowledge of the topic suggested to be able to more fully enjoy the book.

Activity #2
Tell students that prior to your next class meeting they should have done the prereading and reading work for chapters 12-13.

WRITING ASSIGNMENT #2 - *Bud, Not Buddy*

PROMPT
In this book, Bud makes many references to historical people, places, and things. You can read the book and understand it even if you don't have a clue about who or what Bud refers to, but if you take time to learn a little bit about the things he refers to, your reading and understanding will have more depth.

ASSIGNMENT
Each of you will be assigned a person, place or thing Bud refers to in the book. Look in books, magazines and/or encyclopedias to find the information you need. You might be amazed how much information you might find about your topic if you search for it on the web, as well. Just remember that information on the web may or may not be reliable. Check the source.

You will have the remainder of this class time to do your research and begin writing your report. Your written report will be due on _____, but you should be prepared to make a statement giving basic information about your topic in class our next class meeting.

This report doesn't have to be a huge, long and involved thing. Just write a solid composition stating the facts that you found about your topic, so someone who doesn't know anything about it would have a good, basic understanding of who the person was or what the thing was. It should be at least a few paragraphs long but doesn't need to be pages and pages of information.

TOPIC
Write down here the topic you have been assigned.

_____

PREWRITING
Look up your topic in an encyclopedia, book, magazine, on the internet, or from any reliable sources. Write down the name of the source you used and take your notes under that heading. Do this for as many sources as you use, at least two.

Look at the information you found. Decide which things need to be included and which things don't. Line through the things you don't need to include so they don't distract you. Of the things that remain, look for a logical progression of ideas: which things should probably be said first, and in what logical order would the other information follow? Make a little rough outline to remind yourself of where you're going when you write.

DRAFTING
Using your outline and your notes, begin to write your report. Again, group main ideas together in paragraphs, and make the paragraphs follow each other in a logical order from beginning to end.

Bud, Not Buddy Writing Assignment #2 page 2

PROMPT
When you finish the rough draft of your paper, ask a student who sits near you to read it. After reading your rough draft, he/she should tell you what he/she liked best about your work, which parts were difficult to understand, and ways in which your work could be improved. Reread your paper considering your critic's comments, and make the corrections you think are necessary.

PROOFREADING
Do a final proofreading of your paper double-checking your grammar, spelling, organization, and the clarity of your ideas.

RESEARCH TOPICS ASSIGNMENTS - *Bud, Not Buddy*
The chapter number where the reference is made is in ( ) next to the topic.

TOPIC	ASSIGNED TO
JOHN DILLINGER (2)	
BRER RABBIT (2)	
LOUISVILLE SLUGGER (3)	
PAUL BUNYAN (3)	
PAUL ROBESON (3)	
J. EDGAR HOOVER (4)	
PRETTY BOY FLOYD (5)	
HERBERT HOOVER (8)	
RUTH DANDRIDGE (11)	
GEORGE WASHINGTON CARVER (11)	
ROYAL CANADIAN MOUNTED POLICE (12)	
MACHINE GUN KELLY (12)	
AL CAPONE (12)	
PACKARD (12)	
KU KLUX KLAN (12)	
JOHN BROWN (12)	
GRAND CENTRAL STATION (15)	
20,000 LEAGUES UNDER THE SEA (17)	
NIAGARA FALLS (17)	
THE LAST SUPPER (12)	
BABY FACE NELSON (10)	
UNIONS - ORGANIZED LABOR	
ORPHANAGES	
LABOR STRIKE	

LESSON EIGHT

Objectives
1. To review the main ideas and events of chapters 12-13
2. To preview and read chapters 14-15
3. To expose all students to a variety of information about the references Bud makes in the book
4. To evaluate the understanding each student has of the topic assigned

Activity #1
Give students a few minutes to formulate answers for the study guide questions for chapters 12-13 and then discuss the answers to the questions in detail. Write the answers on the board or overhead transparency so students can have the correct answers for study purposes.

Activity #2
Invite each student to tell about his or her topic assigned in the previous class period. This need not be a long and involved report; rather, a report that gives the other students in the class a basic understanding of the person, place or thing Bud referred to in the book. If you are going to hold all students accountable for all of these topics, make a composite list that includes the topic and a sentence or two describing the topic and give each student a copy after the reports are over. (Alternately, students could take notes during the presentations. How you handle this depends on the level of your students.)

Activity #3
Do the pre-reading work for Chapters 14-15. Tell students that this plus the reading of the chapters must be completed prior to the next class period.

LESSON NINE

Objectives
1. To review the main ideas and events in chapters 14-15
2. To give the groups time to work on their topics in chapters 11-15
3. To do the pre-reading and reading work for chapters 16-18

Activity #1

Give students a few minutes to formulate answers for the study guide questions for chapters 14-15, and then discuss the answers to the questions in detail. Write the answers on the board or overhead transparency so students can have the correct answers for study purposes. (Remember the multiple choice format is always available any time you choose to give a quiz instead of doing the review this way.)

Activity #2

Break students into their groups and give them time to work on their assignments for chapters 11-15. Depending on the length of your class period, you might give them a certain number of minutes to work or give them the remainder of the class period. If you give them a certain number of minutes, proceed with Activity #3 after their time is up. If you give them the rest of the class time to do Activity #2, tell them to proceed with previewing and reading chapters 16-18 when they finish with their group work.

Activity #3

Tell students that prior to the next class meeting, they should have done the pre-reading vocabulary, and reading work for chapters 16-18. You could do parts of this as class activity or let students do the whole thing independently, whichever suits your class and your teaching style.

LESSON TEN

Objectives
1. To review the main ideas and events from chapters 16-18
2. To preview and read chapter 19
3. To evaluate students' oral reading skills

Activity # 1

Give students a few minutes to formulate answers for the study guide questions for chapters 16-18, and then discuss the answers to the questions in detail. Write the answers on the board or overhead transparency so students can have the correct answers for study purposes.

Activity #2

Give students about ten to fifteen minutes to preview the study questions and do the prereading vocabulary work for chapter 19.

Activity #3

Have students read chapters 20-23 of *Bud, Not Buddy* out loud in class. You probably know the best way to get readers with your class; pick students at random, ask for volunteers, or use whatever method works best for your group. If you have not yet completed an oral reading evaluation for your students this marking period, this would be a good opportunity to do so. A form is included with this unit for your convenience.

If students do not complete reading chapter 19 in class, they should do so prior to your next class meeting.

LESSON ELEVEN

Objectives
1. To give students the opportunity to practice persuasive writing
2. To get students to analyze information, choose a side, and defend a point

Activity

Distribute Writing Assignment #3. Discuss the directions in detail and give students the remainder of the period to work on this assignment. This assignment could also be done using pairs or small groups to discuss the situation(s) presented prior to writing.

ORAL READING EVALUATION - *Bud, Not Buddy*

Name _____ Class _____ Date _____

SKILL	EXCELLENT	GOOD	AVERAGE	FAIR	POOR
Fluency	5	4	3	2	1
Clarity	5	4	3	2	1
Audibility	5	4	3	2	1
Pronunciation	5	4	3	2	1
_____	5	4	3	2	1
_____	5	4	3	2	1

Total _____   Grade _____

Comments:

WRITING ASSIGNMENT #3 - *Bud, Not Buddy*

PROMPT

When we examined "There's No Place Like America Today!," it was evident that a person's point of view can make a big difference in how something is interpreted. There are many situations in *Bud, Not Buddy* in which point of view plays a role in things.

For example, Mr. and Mrs. Amos really thought Bud was a bad boy. The evidence that they saw caused them to believe that he was a wretched child who should be locked away for their own safety. Bud, on the other hand, thought the Amoses were pretty wretched, and we tend to agree with him because we saw the situation differently from the Amoses, through Bud's narration. But suppose the Amoses were on trial for child abuse. Were their actions justified under the circumstances?

Another example would be when the police would not let the men and boys on the train. The men and boys had no tickets, so the police were there to protect the rights of the railroad company. On the other hand, there was no other way out for them; they just wanted to get out and go find jobs to support their families. From the point of view of the men and boys trying to get on the train, the police were bad guys and the rich railroad company should have let them ride for free. From the point of view of the railroad company, the police were the good guys and the freeloading men and boys were criminals. We experienced the event through Bud's narration, which tended to make us feel like the police were being unfair. But if we stop to think about it, the police were upholding the law, doing their jobs.

The point is that when you read about events or see news broadcasts about them on television, when a friend or relative tells you something, when you receive information from any sources, you have to consider the sources, think about what prejudices or limited point of view they might have which may cause them, perhaps unintentionally, to give you slanted or biased information. Have you read *Nothing But The Truth* by Avi? There are a lot of point of view issues in that book, too.

ASSIGNMENT

Your assignment is to consider one of the two examples above (the Amoses or the train incident), choose the side of one of the participants, and persuade me that their point of view was the correct one. Persuade me that The Amoses were justified in sending Bud to the shed **OR** that Bud was right and the Amoses were wretched people **OR** that the men and boys trying to get on the train were justified and the police or railroad company should have let them on **OR** the railroad company and the police were right to try to keep the men and boys off of the train. Choose ONE of these to defend.

PRE-WRITING

Think for a few minutes about the two different situations and the points of view of each of the participants. Which one do you feel you can most strongly defend? Can't decide? Pull out a sheet of paper, put 4 columns on it, and label each one Amoses, Bud, Police, or Men. Under each label, write down as many reasons as you can FOR that point of view. Whichever one you have the most good reasons for is the one you should write about.

Bud, Not Buddy Writing Assignment #3 page 2

DRAFTING

Write a short introductory paragraph in which you state your position. Choose your three or four best reasons for your position from the column in the pre-writing exercise. Write one paragraph for each reason. State the complete reason as the topic sentence then explain or give examples to support it in the rest of the paragraph. Do that for each reason. Save your strongest reason for last. Write a short concluding paragraph.

PROMPT

When you finish the rough draft of your paper, ask a student who sits near you to read it. After reading your rough draft, he/she should tell you what he/she liked best about your work, which parts were difficult to understand, and ways in which your work could be improved. Reread your paper considering your critic's comments, and make the corrections you think are necessary.

PROOFREADING

Do a final proofreading of your paper double-checking your grammar, spelling, organization, and the clarity of your ideas.

LESSON TWELVE

Objective
   To give students time to complete their group work projects

Activity
   Give students this class time to get together in their groups to complete their group projects and prepare their reports.

   NOTE: Remember each group will need copies made of its compiled list so each class member can have a copy. Some students will be able to run their own copies from their computers at home, but others may need your assistance or the use of school copiers.

LESSONS THIRTEEN THROUGH FIFTEEN

Objectives
   1. To discuss, in depth, the topics assigned for the group projects so students will have a deeper understanding of this novel
   2. To evaluate students' group work
   3. To give students a sense of accomplishment by sharing their work with their classmates, being "teacher" for their topics, and knowing that the detailed work that they did brought something useful to the class

Activity
   Spend these class periods doing the group report presentations and using those as a springboard to discuss the many details and issues surrounding each topic. You may not need three class periods, or you may need more. Adjust the schedule according to your class's needs.

LESSONS SIXTEEN AND SEVENTEEN

Objective
> To discuss many points and issues relating to *Bud, Not Buddy* which were not covered in the group presentation discussions

Activity #1
> Choose the questions from the Extra Discussion Questions/Writing Assignments which seem most appropriate for your students. A class discussion of these questions is most effective if students have been given the opportunity to formulate answers to the questions prior to the discussion. To this end, you may either have all the students formulate answers to all the questions, divide your class into groups and assign one or more questions to each group, or you could assign one question to each student in your class. The option you choose will make a difference in the amount of class time needed for this activity.

Activity #2
> After students have had ample time to formulate answers to the questions, begin your class discussion of the questions and the ideas presented by the questions. Be sure students take notes during the discussion so they have information to study for the unit test.

EXTRA WRITING ASSIGNMENTS/DISCUSSION QUESTIONS - *Bud, Not Buddy*

Interpretation

1. From what point of view is *Bud, Not Buddy* written? What advantages did using that point of view give the author?

2. If you were to rewrite *Bud, Not Buddy* as a play, where would you start and end each act? Explain why.

3. Where is the climax of the story? Explain your choice.

4. What are the main conflicts in the novel? Are they all resolved? If so, how? If not, why not?

5. List the people who helped Bud along his way and tell what each person did for him.

6. Give three examples of Bud's practical nature and common sense.

7. Give three examples of times that Bud's imagination added interest to the book.

Critical

8. The library and librarians played an important role in the book. Explain how they were used.

9. Explain the importance of the setting in *Bud, Not Buddy*. Could this story have been set in a different time and place and still have the same effect?

10. Characterize Christopher Paul Curtis's style of writing. How does it contribute to the value of the novel?

11. Early in the story Bud said, "Todd Amos was hitting me so hard and fast that I knew that the blood squirting out of my nose was only the beginning of a whole long list of bad things that were about to happen to me." Was that actually true? Did this event and statement foreshadow a "whole long list of bad things" that happened to Bud in the rest of the book?

12. Why do people always want to call Bud "Buddy"? Explain why that is an important point in the book., and explain why Bud insists on being called "Bud," not "Buddy."

13. Explain the relationship between Momma and Herman E. Calloway.

14. Are the characters in *Bud, Not Buddy* stereotypes? If so, explain why Christopher Paul Curtis used stereotypes. If not, explain how the characters merit individuality.

15. Compare and contrast Deza and Buddy.

Bud, Not Buddy Extra Discussion Questions page 2

16. How do we know Momma was a good mother?

17. Describe Momma. Take all the clues we get about her through the book and tell who she was.

18. "I can see how Momma was so wrong. She was wrong because she probably should've told me the things she thought I was too young to hear, because now that she's gone, I'll never know what they were. Even if I was too young back then, I could've rememorized them and used them when I did need help, like right now." Was Momma wrong?

19. What is the importance of each of the following: the suitcase(s), the flyers, the blanket, and the stones?

20. Mrs. Sleet's little girl, Kim, sang a song and so did Deza Malone. Explain the significance of each of their songs.

21. Compare and contrast Miss Thomas and Momma.

22. Compare and contrast Lefty and Herman E. Calloway.

23. Compare and contrast life today with life of the era in *Bud, Not Buddy*.

24. Explain what use each of these people had in the author's development of the plot and themes of the book: the librarian, Miss Hill, the pretend family at the mission, Jerry, Bugs, the Amoses, the woman in Hooverville, Deza Malone, the police at the train, Mrs. Sleet, Lefty Lewis, Jimmy, Steady Eddie, and Miss Thomas.

Personal Response

25. Did you enjoy reading *Bud, Not Buddy*? Why or why not?

26. Would you like to have Buddy as a friend? Why or why not?

27. Who helped Buddy the most? Justify your answer.

28. What was the most crucial event that enabled Bud to get to his real family? Explain why.

29. Was Herman E. Calloway just a grumpy, mean, old man, or not? Explain your answer.

30. What was the best part of the book? Why?

31. Do you think the rest of Bud's life will be as exciting and interesting as this part? Why or why not?

QUOTATIONS WORKSHEET
Bud, Not Buddy

1. "It was like something was telling me there was a message for me on this flyer but I didn't have the decoder ring to read what it was." (Chapter 1)

2. "I knew that the blood squirting out of my nose was only the beginning of a whole long list of bad things that were about to happen to me." (Chapter 2)

3. "If I was like a normal kid, I would've busted out crying." (Chapter 2)

4. "There comes a time when you're losing a fight that it just doesn't make sense to keep on fighting. It's not that you're being a quitter, it's just that you've got the sense to know when enough is enough." (Chapter 2)

5. "Just like there's a time that a smart person know enough is enough, there's a time when you know you've got to fight." (Chapter 3)

6. "Most folks don't have sense enough to carry a blanket around with them, but you never know when you might be sleeping under a Christmas tree at the library so I always keep mine handy." (Chapter 5)

7. "A bud is a flower-to-be. A flower-in-waiting. Waiting for just the right warmth and care to open up. It's a little fist of love waiting to unfold and be seen by the world. And that's you." (Chapter 5)

8. ". . . no matter how bad things look to you, no matter how dark the night, when one door closes, don't worry, because another door opens." (Chapter 5)

9. "And there were more people sitting around that I first thought, too, mostly it was men and big boys, but there were a couple of women every now and then and a kid or two. They were all the colors you could think of, black, white and brown, but the fire made everyone look like there were different shades of orange. There were dark orange folks sitting next to medium orange folks sitting next to light orange folks." (Chapter 8)

10. "I promise you suitcase will be safe here." I remembered the Amoses had promised the same thing." (Chapter 8)

11. [Bud has just told Deza that it was okay that his mother had died.] "No it's not, and you should quit pretending that it is." [Bud replies,] "Who said I'm pretending anything?" (Chapter 8)

12. "Thank you very much, but we're white people. We ain't in need of a handout." (Chapter 8)

Bud, Not Buddy Quotations page 2

13. "But I guess you're different, aren't you, Bud? I guess you sort of carry your family around inside of you, huh?" [Bud replies,] "I guess I do. Inside my suitcase, too." (Chapter 8)

14. "I started dreaming about the man with the giant fiddle. He was walking away and I kept calling him but he couldn't look back. Then the dream got a lot better, I turned away from were Herman E. Calloway was and there stood Deza Malone. I told her, 'I really like your dimple.' She laughed and said, 'See you in seven years.'" (Chapter 8)

15. "This is America, boys, you're sounding like a bunch of Commies, you know I can't let you on this train. I got kids to feed, too, and I'd lose my job." (Chapter 8)

16. "But it was like a miracle, the flyer flipped over three times and landed right in my hand. I slowed down and put it in my pocket." (Chapter 8)

17. "Man, this is one tough suitcase, you couldn't even tell what it had been through, it still looked exactly the same." (Chapter 8)

18. "Maybe someone was trying to tell me something, what with me missing the train and the blue flyer floating back to me, maybe Deza Malone was right. Maybe I should stay here in Flint." (Chapter 8)

19. "It's funny how ideas are, in a lot of ways they're just like seeds. Both of them start real, real small, and then . . . woop, zoop, sloop . . . before you can say Jack Robinson they've gone and grown a lot bigger than you ever thought they could." (Chapter 9)

20. "Momma must've known she wasn't going to be around too long and was trying to leave me a message about who my daddy was and why she couldn't never talk about him." (Chapter 9)

21. "I wonder how grown folks know so doggone much by just looking at you." (Chapter 10)

22. ". . . before my brain could stop it my stomach told the rest of me to slide my suitcase deeper into the weeds and walk out." (Chapter 10)

23. "Sometimes it's terrible to have been brought up proper." (Chapter 11)

24. "We hadn't been driving for a minute before he started asking a whole slew of questions. Questions that I had to be very careful about giving the right answers to." (Chapter 11)

25. "I sucked in a jumbo gulp of air and opened the front door again. This time I pushed the second set of doors open and walked in." (Chapter 12)

Bud, Not Buddy Quotations page 3

26. "I kept my eyes closed and smiled. I knew I was going to be safe, because I'd never heard of a vampire that could drive a car and I'd never seen one that had such a good sense of humor. Besides, I kept my jackknife open under my leg . . . ." (Chapter 11)

27. "It was the exact same thought I'd had when I got whipped by Toddy boy! Only two folks with the same blood would think them just alike! I sucked in a big gulp of air, got a good grip on my suitcase and walked into the light of the stage." (Chapter 12)

28. "I put this Thug guy on my list of people not to pay any mind to. Herman E. Calloway seemed like the kind of person that would rather get bit in the behind by a snaggletooth mule than have somebody give him a kiss." (Chapter 13)

29. "All of a sudden I knew that of all the places in the world that I'd ever been in this was the one. That of all the people I'd ever met these were the ones. This was where I was supposed to be." (Chapter 14)

30. "Go ahead and cry, Bud, you're home." (Chapter 14)

31. "Herman E. Calloway didn't have to worry, I was a liar, not a thief." (Chapter 15)

32. "I took in a deep, deep breath and it felt like I was sleeping with my own blanket wrapped around my head. I took in a couple more deep breaths and I could hear Momma starting to read another story to me." (Chapter 15)

33. "That's what I need to know, are you attached to the suitcase, or is it the things inside that are important?" [Bud replied,] "I'd never thought about that before, I'd always thought of the suitcase and the things inside together." (Chapter 16)

34. ". . . Herman E. Calloway didn't even know how much fun I was having. Making somebody work hard isn't as easy as it looks, some folks are good at it and some folks aren't." (Chapter 17)

35. "I'd finally put her somewhere where she wanted to be, back in her own bedroom, back amongst all her horses." (Chapter 19)

36. "Deza Malone was right, I was carrying Momma inside me and there wasn't anyone or anything that could take away from that or add to it either." (Chapter 19)

38. "I could tell those were the squeaks and squawks of one door closing and another one opening." (Chapter 19)

LESSON EIGHTEEN

<u>Objective</u>
To review all of the vocabulary work done in this unit

<u>Activity</u>
Choose one (or more) of the vocabulary review activities listed below and spend your class period as directed in the activity. Some of the materials for these review activities are located in the Extra Activities in this unit.

VOCABULARY REVIEW ACTIVITIES

1. Divide your class into two teams and have an old-fashioned spelling or definition bee.

2. Give each of your students (or students in groups of two, three or four) a *Bud, Not Buddy* Vocabulary Word Search Puzzle. The person (group) to find all of the vocabulary words in the puzzle first wins.

3. Give students a *Bud, Not Buddy* Vocabulary Word Search Puzzle without the word list. The person or group to find the most vocabulary words in the puzzle wins.

4. Use a *Bud, Not Buddy* Vocabulary Crossword Puzzle. Put the puzzle onto a transparency on the overhead projector (so everyone can see it), and do the puzzle together as a class.

5. Give students a *Bud, Not Buddy* Vocabulary Matching Worksheet to do.

6. Divide your class into two teams. Use *Bud, Not Buddy* vocabulary words with their letters jumbled as a word list. Student 1 from Team A faces off against Student 1 from Team B. You write the first jumbled word on the board. The first student (1A or 1B) to unscramble the word wins the chance for his/her team to score points. If 1A wins the jumble, go to student 2A and give him/her a definition. He/she must give you the correct spelling of the vocabulary word which fits that definition. If he/she does, Team A scores a point, and you give student 3A a definition for which you expect a correctly spelled matching vocabulary word. Continue giving Team A definitions until some team member makes an incorrect response. An incorrect response sends the game back to the jumbled-word face off, this time with students 2A and 2B. Instead of repeating giving definitions to the first few students of each team, continue with the student after the one who gave the last incorrect response on the team. For example, if Team B wins the jumbled-word face-off, and student 5B gave the last incorrect answer for Team B, you would start this round of definition questions with student 6B, and so on. The team with the most points wins!

7. Have students write a story in which they correctly use as many vocabulary words as possible. Have students read their compositions orally! Post the most original compositions on your bulletin board!

LESSON NINETEEN

<u>Objective</u>
　　To review the main ideas presented in *Bud, Not Buddy*

<u>Activity #1</u>
　　Choose one of the review games/activities included in this guide and spend your class period as outlined there. Some materials for these activities are located in the Unit Resource Materials section of this LitPlan.

<u>Activity #2</u>
　　Remind students that the Unit Test will be in the next class meeting. Stress the review of the study guides and their class notes as a last minute, brush-up review for homework.

REVIEW GAMES/ACTIVITIES - *Bud, Not Buddy*

1. Ask the class to make up a unit test for *Bud, Not Buddy*. The test should have 4 sections: matching, true/false, short answer, and essay. Students may use 1/2 period to make the test and then swap papers and use the other 1/2 class period to take a test a classmate has devised. (open book) You may want to use the unit test included in this guide or take questions from the students' unit tests to formulate your own test.

2. Take 1/2 period for students to make up true and false questions (including the answers). Collect the papers and divide the class into two teams. Draw a big tic-tac-toe board on the chalk board. Make one team X and one team O. Ask questions to each side, giving each student one turn. If the question is answered correctly, that students' team's letter (X or O) is placed in the box. If the answer is incorrect, no mark is placed in the box. The object is to get three marks in a row like tic-tac-toe. You may want to keep track of the number of games won for each team.

3. Take 1/2 period for students to make up questions (true/false and short answer). Collect the questions. Divide the class into two teams. You'll alternate asking questions to individual members of teams A & B (like in a spelling bee). The question keeps going from A to B until it is correctly answered, then a new question is asked. A correct answer does not allow the team to get another question. Correct answers are +2 points; incorrect answers are -1 point.

4. Have students pair up and quiz each other from their study guides and class notes.

5. Give students a *Bud, Not Buddy* crossword puzzle to complete.

6. Divide your class into two teams. Use *Bud, Not Buddy* crossword words with their letters jumbled as a word list. Student 1 from Team A faces off against Student 1 from Team B. You write the first jumbled word on the board. The first student (1A or 1B) to unscramble the word wins the chance for his/her team to score points. If 1A wins the jumble, go to student 2A and give him/her a clue. He/she must give you the correct word which matches that clue. If he/she does, Team A scores a point, and you give student 3A a clue for which you expect another correct response. Continue giving Team A clues until some team member makes an incorrect response. An incorrect response sends the game back to the jumbled-word face off, this time with students 2A and 2B. Instead of repeating giving clues to the first few students of each team, continue with the student after the one who gave the last incorrect response on the team. For example, if Team B wins the jumbled-word face-off, and student 5B gave the last incorrect answer for Team B, you would start this round of clue questions with student 6B, and so on. The team with the most points wins!

UNIT TESTS

SHORT ANSWER UNIT TEST 1 - *Bud, Not Buddy*

I. Matching/Identify

_____ 1. Caldwell   A. looked unhappy in the picture at the Miss B. Gotten Moon Park

_____ 2. Todd Amos   B. kissed Bud after washing dishes in Hooverville

_____ 3. Momma   C. gave Bud a ride to Grand Rapids

_____ 4. Calloway   D. Bud's last name

_____ 5. Bugs   E. shoved a pencil up Bud's nose

_____ 6. Clarence   F. gave Bud a new case

_____ 7. Deza   G. Lefty's daughter

_____ 8. Lefty   H. left Hooverville on the train headed west

_____ 9. Steady Eddie   I. vocal stylist who took care of Bud

_____ 10. Miss Thomas   J. Bud's grandfather's last name

_____ 11. Sweet Pea   K. Bud's pretend name

_____ 12. Mrs. Sleet   L. restaurant where the band went

II. Short Answer

1. What was printed on the blue flyer? Why was it special?

2. What was Bud's revenge plan against the Amoses?

3. What did Bud's use of his blanket tell us about him?

Bud, Not Buddy Short Answer Unit Test 1 Page 2

4. What did Momma tell Bud about his name?

5. What did Momma tell Bud about doors?

6. What did Bud know about the library door's closing?

7. Why did Bud start wondering if going to California was the right thing to do?

8. Why did Bud miss the train from Hooverville?

9. How are ideas like seeds?

10. Why did Bud tell the man he had run away from Grand Rapids?

11. Why did Bud say that it's terrible to have been brought up proper?

12. Why did Bud sleep so well in the car and through that first night with Mr. Lewis?

Bud, Not Buddy Short Answer Unit Test 1 Page 3

13. What was Bud's reason for thinking it was okay to lie to an adult but not to a kid?

14. What warning did Herman E. Calloway give Bud about snooping around the house? What was Bud's reaction to Herman E. Calloway's warning?

15. What name did Bud get? Why?

16. What was the answer to Bud's question, "Why does he always keep one white guy in the band?"

17. What finally convinced Herman E. Calloway that Bud might be his relative?

18. What was written on the stones, and why was it written on them?

Bud, Not Buddy Short Answer Unit Test 1 Page 4

III. Quotations

1. "It was like something was telling me there was a message for me on this flyer but I didn't have the decoder ring to read what it was." What did the message on the flyer turn out to be?

2. "I promise you suitcase will be safe here." I remembered the Amoses had promised the same thing." This quote was from Bud's Hooverville experiences. Compare/contrast how the Hoovervillians treated his suitcase with how the Amoses did. What is the message for us there?

3. "Maybe someone was trying to tell me something, what with me missing the train and the blue flyer floating back to me. . ." What was someone trying to tell Bud?

4. "It's funny how ideas are, in a lot of ways they're just like seeds. Both of them start real, real small, and then . . . woop, zoop, sloop . . . before you can say Jack Robinson they've gone and grown a lot bigger than you ever thought they could." What was the idea that Bud was talking about here?

5. "I wonder how grown folks know so doggone much by just looking at you." To what was Bud referring when he thought this, and how *do* grown folks know?

6. "Sometimes it's terrible to have been brought up proper." Why did Bud say this?

Bud, Not Buddy Short Answer Unit Test 1 Page 5

7. "We hadn't been driving for a minute before he started asking a whole slew of questions. Questions that I had to be very careful about giving the right answers to." What did this tell us about Bud?

8. "Go ahead and cry, Bud, you're home." Who said this to Bud?

9. "Herman E. Calloway didn't have to worry, I was a liar, not a thief." Why was Herman E. Calloway worried, and what does this quote tell us about Bud?

10. "I took in a deep, deep breath and it felt like I was sleeping with my own blanket wrapped around my head. I took in a couple more deep breaths and I could hear Momma starting to read another story to me." Where was Bud? Why did he feel like he was sleeping with his own blanket around his head?

11. "That's what I need to know, are you attached to the suitcase, or is it the things inside that are important?" [Bud replied,] "I'd never thought about that before, I'd always thought of the suitcase and the things inside together." Why is this quote significant?

12. "I'd finally put her somewhere where she wanted to be, back in her own bedroom, back amongst all her horses." Explain the significance of this action.

Bud, Not Buddy Short Answer Unit Test 1 Page 6

IV. Essay

Trace the theme of doors closing and opening through the book *Bud, Not Buddy*. Give specific examples.

Bud, Not Buddy Short Answer Unit Test 1 Page 7

IV. Vocabulary

    Listen to the vocabulary words and spell them. After you have spelled all the words, go back and write down the definitions.

    1.

    2.

    3.

    4.

    5.

    6.

    7.

    8.

    9.

    10.

KEY: SHORT ANSWER UNIT TEST #1 - *Bud, Not Buddy*

I. Matching/Identify

D 1. Caldwell   A. looked unhappy in the picture at the Miss B. Gotten Moon Park

E 2. Todd Amos   B. kissed Bud after washing dishes in Hooverville

A 3. Momma   C. gave Bud a ride to Grand Rapids

J 4. Calloway   D. Bud's last name

H 5. Bugs   E. shoved a pencil up Bud's nose

K 6. Clarence   F. gave Bud a new case

B 7. Deza   G. Lefty's daughter

C 8. Lefty   H. left Hooverville on the train headed west

F 9. Steady Eddie   I. vocal stylist who took care of Bud

I 10. Miss Thomas   J. Bud's grandfather's last name

L 11. Sweet Pea   K. Bud's pretend name

G 12. Mrs. Sleet   L. restaurant where the band went

II. Short Answer

1. What was printed on the blue flyer? Why was it special?
   The paper was a flyer advertising Herman E. Calloway and the Dusky Devastators of the Depression, with a picture of a man standing next to a giant fiddle. Bud thought the man might be his father.

2. What was Bud's revenge plan against the Amoses?
   He hid the gun from the Amoses so they couldn't use it against him if things went wrong with his revenge plan. Then, he poured water on Todd's pajama pants while Todd was sleeping, inducing the desired effect of Todd's wetting the bed.

3. What did Bud's use of his blanket tell us about him?
   First, he's smart enough to recognize the value of a blanket and to carry one with him. Also, that he folds it neatly in his suitcase to keep things in place shows us he is smart, neat and careful with his things.

4. What did Momma tell Bud about his name?
    She told him she named him Bud, not Buddy. "A bud is a flower-to-be. A flower in waiting. Waiting for just the right warmth and care to open it up. A little fist of love waiting to unfold and be seen by the world."

5. What did Momma tell Bud about doors?
    "No matter how bad things look to you, no matter how dark the night, when one door closes, don't worry, because another door opens."

6. What did Bud know about the library door's closing?
    "That library door closing after I walked out was the exact kind of door Momma had told me about. I knew that since it had closed the next one was about to open."

7. Why did Bud start wondering if going to California was the right thing to do?
    He was thinking that "Deza's momma was right, someone who doesn't know who their family is, is like dust blowing around in a storm. . . ." He thought it was more likely he could find his own family closer to Flint than in California.

8. Why did Bud miss the train from Hooverville?
    He ran back to get his blue flyer he had left at the shack in Hooverville. When he returned and tried to catch the train, he threw the suitcase to Bugs, but the blue flyer he had hastily slipped under the twine on his suitcase fell out. Bud stopped to get it and put it in his pocket, and the delay was just enough to keep him from being able to catch the train.

9. How are ideas like seeds?
    "Both of them start real, real small and then . . . woop, zoop, sloop . . . before you can say Jack Robinson they've gone and grown a lot bigger than you ever thought they could."

10. Why did Bud tell the man he had run away from Grand Rapids?
    Bud knew that if he told the man he was from Flint, the man would take him back to Flint. Bud wanted to go to Grand Rapids, so he thought that if he told the man he was from Grand Rapids, the man would take him there.

11. Why did Bud say that it's terrible to have been brought up proper?
    When the grown-up man told him to roll down the window, he did it out of obedience to the grown-up.

12. Why did Bud sleep so well in the car and through that first night with Mr. Lewis?
    He felt safe with someone who cared about him and would take him to Herman E. Calloway. He could relax.

13. What was Bud's reason for thinking it was okay to lie to an adult but not to a kid?
    "Most times adults want to hear something that lets them take their attention off you and put it on something else. That makes it easy and not too bad to lie to them. . . . Most times kids really do want to know what they're asking you." So it would be more wrong to lie to someone who really wants to know.

14. What warning did Herman E. Calloway give Bud about snooping around the house? What was Bud's reaction to Herman E. Calloway's warning?

   Herman E. Calloway said, "I know where every single thing belongs and I can tell right away when something's missing. I've got little secret bells all over everything and when something's stolen the bell goes off and only I can hear it, so watch your step."
   Bud' reaction was, ". . . nothing makes you want to steal something more than having somebody who doesn't even know you're honest telling you not to steal. Herman E. Calloway didn't have to worry, I was a liar, not a thief."

15. What name did Bud get? Why?

   Bud's band name was Sleepy LaBone because he slept so late in the morning and he was skinny.

16. What was the answer to Bud's question, "Why does he always keep one white guy in the band?"

   It was against the law for a Negro to own property where the Log Cabin is, so Mr. Calloway put it in Deed's name. Also, Eddie explained that, ". . . a lot of times we get gigs playing polkas and waltzes and a lot of these white folks wouldn't hire us if they knew we were a Negro band so Deed goes out and sets up everything."

17. What finally convinced Herman E. Calloway that Bud might be his relative?

   Bud produced the stones that Herman Calloway had sent to Bud's mother, HEC's daughter.

18. What was written on the stones, and why was it written on them?

   Before Herman Calloway went to Chicago to play a job when his daughter was four or five years old, he asked her what she wanted him to bring back for her. She asked for a rock. So, everywhere HEC went after that, he brought her a rock with the city and date written on it.

III. Quotations

1. "It was like something was telling me there was a message for me on this flyer but I didn't have the decoder ring to read what it was." What did the message on the flyer turn out to be?

   It turned out that Herman E. Calloway was Bud's grandfather, a band leader and performer in Grand Rapids.

2. "I promise you suitcase will be safe here." I remembered the Amoses had promised the same thing." This quote was from Bud's Hooverville experiences. Compare/contrast how the Hoovervillians treated his suitcase with how the Amoses did. What is the message for us there?

   The Amoses promised not to look in his suitcase, but did open it and look in it. The Hoovervillians promised not to look in his suitcase and kept their promise. The Amoses were "approved" by the home, by society, to be upright and take care of Bud. The Hoovervillians were supposedly the outcasts, the worst part of society. However, the Hoovervillians were in many ways far more honorable and better people than the Amoses. The message is that you can't judge a book by its cover.

3. "Maybe someone was trying to tell me something, what with me missing the train and the blue flyer floating back to me. . ." What was someone trying to tell Bud?
    The message for Bud was that he should stay nearer to home to find his relatives rather than going west to make his own way alone.

4. "It's funny how ideas are, in a lot of ways they're just like seeds. Both of them start real, real small, and then . . . woop, zoop, sloop . . . before you can say Jack Robinson they've gone and grown a lot bigger than you ever thought they could." What was the idea that Bud was talking about here?
    He was talking about the idea that Herman E. Calloway was his father.

5. "I wonder how grown folks know so doggone much by just looking at you." To what was Bud referring when he thought this, and how *do* grown folks know?
    Bud was referring to Lefty's knowing he was hungry and from Flint. Grown folks know because they have experience in looking for and interpreting the clues surrounding the situation.

6. "Sometimes it's terrible to have been brought up proper." Why did Bud say this?
    He didn't want to stop and roll down the window and talk to Lefty, but because he was brought up proper, his automatic response was to be obedient. Sometimes he thought it would certainly make life easier if he didn't have to do the right thing.

7. "We hadn't been driving for a minute before he started asking a whole slew of questions. Questions that I had to be very careful about giving the right answers to." What did this tell us about Bud?
    Bud was being cautious on two levels. First, he was careful because the man asking the questions was a stranger. He had sense enough to know that you had to be careful when talking to strangers. Also, though, he had to be careful to give the answers that would get him what he wanted/needed. He was weaving a fine line between the truth and lies.

8. "Go ahead and cry, Bud, you're home." Who said this to Bud?
    Miss Thomas did.

9. "Herman E. Calloway didn't have to worry, I was a liar, not a thief." Why was Herman E. Calloway worried, and what does this quote tell us about Bud?
    Herman E. Calloway had the same cautious nature Bud did. He didn't know this kid and he was afraid Bud would carry away anything of value. Also, he was obviously not very good with children–at least not with his own child–and perhaps having a child in the house again, in particular in his daughter's room, dredged up bad feelings of guilt and sadness, making him overly gruff. Bud's statement tells us that he didn't know or understand why Herman E. Calloway threatened him, but more importantly that Bud knows himself. He knows which fault is his and readily admits it.

10. "I took in a deep, deep breath and it felt like I was sleeping with my own blanket wrapped around my head. I took in a couple more deep breaths and I could hear Momma starting to read another story to me." Where was Bud? Why did he feel like he was sleeping with his own blanket around his head?

Bud was in his mother's room, but he doesn't know it's his mother's room yet. Bud's blanket has always symbolized his mother, her care of him, and their relationship. We know he has the feeling of his blanket wrapped around his head because he is in his mother's room, surrounded by her things.

11. "That's what I need to know, are you attached to the suitcase, or is it the things inside that are important?" [Bud replied,] "I'd never thought about that before, I'd always thought of the suitcase and the things inside together." Why is this quote significant?

    It is the beginning of Bud's separation from the items in the suitcase. Until now he has carried his family with him both in himself and in the suitcase. Here is where the separation begins; the *things* in the suitcase can go into another box; they are one step removed from him as he begins to associate with and immerse himself in his new, real family. Eventually, he will separate himself totally from the suitcase and all the things inside when he crosses through that final open door in the book and begins to live his life fully knowing he is with his real family.

12. "I'd finally put her somewhere where she wanted to be, back in her own bedroom, back amongst all her horses." Explain the significance of this action.

    Both Bud and Momma have come home and can be at peace. His putting her picture on the wall where it "belonged" is his final separation with the *things* in the suitcase. Everything is where it now belongs and he is fully able to go forward with his life.

IV. Essay

Trace the theme of doors closing and opening through the book *Bud, Not Buddy*. Give specific examples.

IV. Vocabulary

Choose ten of the vocabulary words to dictate to your class for this section of the test.

SHORT ANSWER UNIT TEST 2 - *Bud, Not Buddy*

I. Matching/Identify

_____ 1. Caldwell   A. Lefty's daughter

_____ 2. Todd Amos   B. Bud's grandfather's last name

_____ 3. Momma   C. gave Bud a ride to Grand Rapids

_____ 4. Calloway   D. looked unhappy in the picture at the Miss B. Gotten Moon Park

_____ 5. Bugs   E. shoved a pencil up Bud's nose

_____ 6. Clarence   F. left Hooverville on the train headed west

_____ 7. Deza   G. Bud's last name

_____ 8. Lefty   H. kissed Bud after washing dishes in Hooverville

_____ 9. Steady Eddie   I. Bud's pretend name

_____ 10. Miss Thomas   J. restaurant where the band went

_____ 11. Sweet Pea   K. gave Bud a new case

_____ 12. Mrs. Sleet   L. vocal stylist who took care of Bud

II. Short Answer

1. According to Bud, did he have a better foster family assignment than Jerry did? Explain. Was he right?

2. Why did Bud get mad after he got out of the shed?

3. What did Bud's use of his blanket tell us about him? What does the blanket symbolize?

Bud, Not Buddy Short Answer Unit Test 2 Page 2

4. Why was Bud's name "Bud," not "Buddy"?

5. Why did the author include the part about Bud's pretend family at the mission?

6. The library and librarian(s) were a significant part of the book. How were they used?

7. The white people with the sick baby at Hooverville were very minor characters but were significant. Why?

8. How did the flyer lead Bud to his real home?

9. Why did Bud tell Lefty that he had run away from Grand Rapids? Did it work?

10. Give two examples of Bud's being smart and cautious.

Bud, Not Buddy Short Answer Unit Test 2 Page 3

11. Give two examples of how we know Momma was a good mother.

12. Why did Lefty tell Bud to come see him if he decided to travel again?

13. What was Bud's first impression of Herman E. Calloway? Was it accurate?

14. What hit Bud as hard as Snaggletooth MacNevin had smacked Herman E. Calloway?

15. Give two examples of Bud's practical nature and common sense in being able to fend for himself?

16. What finally convinced Herman E. Calloway that Bud might be his relative? What was the final proof that Bud's mother and Herman's daughter were one and the same?

17. Why didn't Bud need his suitcase items anymore? What did he do with the flyers, stones, and picture of his mother?

18. What did the squeaks and squawks of the saxophone sound like to Bud?

Bud, Not Buddy Short Answer Unit Test 2 Page 4

III. REAL PEOPLE, PLACES & THINGS

Choose **five** of these people, places or things that Bud mentions in the book and identify them:

John Dillinger	Louisville Slugger	Baby Face Nelson	Last Supper
Paul Bunyan	Paul Robeson	J. Edgar Hoover	Pretty Boy Floyd
Herbert Hoover	Ruth Dandridge	Machine Gun Kelly	Al Capone
Ku Klux Klan	Packard	John Brown	Organized Labor

Bud, Not Buddy Short Answer Unit Test 2 page 5

IV. Vocabulary

Listen to the vocabulary words and spell them. After you have spelled all the words, go back and write down the definitions.

1.

2.

3.

4.

5.

6.

7.

8.

9.

10.

KEY: SHORT ANSWER UNIT TEST 2 - *Bud, Not Buddy*

I. Matching/Identify

G 1. Caldwell   A. Lefty's daughter

E 2. Todd Amos   B. Bud's grandfather's last name

D 3. Momma   C. gave Bud a ride to Grand Rapids

B 4. Calloway   D. looked unhappy in the picture at the Miss B. Gotten Moon Park

F 5. Bugs   E. shoved a pencil up Bud's nose

I 6. Clarence   F. left Hooverville on the train headed west

H 7. Deza   G. Bud's last name

C 8. Lefty   H. kissed Bud after washing dishes in Hooverville

K 9. Steady Eddie   I. Bud's pretend name

L 10. Miss Thomas   J. restaurant where the band went

J 11. Sweet Pea   K. gave Bud a new case

A 12. Mrs. Sleet   L. vocal stylist who took care of Bud

II. Short Answer

1. According to Bud, did he have a better foster family assignment than Jerry did? Explain. Was he right?

   Bud said that Jerry had a better assignment. He said, "I know being in a house with three girls sounds terrible, Jerry, but it's a lot better than being with a boy who's a couple of years older than you. . . . A older boy is going to want to fight, but those little girls are going to treat you real good." He was right.

2. Why did Bud get mad after he got out of the shed?

   He was mad at the Amos family but mostly mad at himself for believing there was a vampire in the shed and for getting trapped in a situation where there wasn't anyone who cared what happened to him.

3. What did Bud's use of his blanket tell us about him? What does the blanket symbolize?

   First, he's smart enough to recognize the value of a blanket and to carry one with him. Also, that he folds it neatly in his suitcase to keep things in place shows us he is smart, neat and careful with his things. It symbolizes his mother and her care of him.

4. Why was Bud's name "Bud," not "Buddy."
   His mother told him she named him Bud, not Buddy. "A bud is a flower-to-be. A flower in waiting. Waiting for just the right warmth and care to open it up. A little fist of love waiting to unfold and be seen by the world."

5. Why did the author include the part about Bud's pretend family at the mission?
   They were another type of people who were low on the social ladder but, in their own, rough way, were very kind and helped him. The events at the mission gave the author another venue for showing the value of every person regardless of social class and the insensitive treatment the poor and homeless often get from the rest of society.

6. The library and librarian(s) were a significant part of the book. How were they used?
   The library was a substitute home and the librarian(s) were mother-like. Bud got help, food, and shelter there. It was significant that he and his mother used to go there together.

7. The white people with the sick baby at Hooverville were very minor characters but were significant. Why?
   They were too proud to accept help from people they thought were beneath their station in life. They showed the depth of prejudice in our society in that era.

8. How did the flyer lead Bud to his real home?
   He first got the idea that Herman E. Calloway was his father from the flyer. Later he left the flyer in Hooverville and had to go back for it. In his haste, he just stuck it under the string instead of carefully putting it back where it belonged as he always did. When he ran to get the train, the flyer flew out from under the string, delaying him just enough that he missed the train, so he stayed in Flint instead of going west. The flyer gave him information that set him towards Grand Rapids.

9. Why did Bud tell Lefty that he had run away from Grand Rapids? Did it work?
   Bud knew that if he said he was from Flint, Lefty would take him back to Flint. Bud wanted to go to Grand Rapids, so he thought that if he said he was from Grand Rapids, Lefty would take him there. Yes, it worked!

10. Give two examples of Bud's being smart and cautious.
    There are many examples of this in the book. Any examples that fit are right.

11. Give two examples of how we know Momma was a good mother.
    Again, there are many examples to choose from. Any examples that fit are right.

12. Why did Lefty tell Bud to come see him if he decided to travel again?
    He liked Bud and would want to take care of him so no harm would come to him.

13. What was Bud's first impression of Herman E. Calloway? Was it accurate?
    Bud thought he "seemed like he was going to be hard to get along with." Yes, but we come to understand why Herman E. Calloway seemed to be hard to get along with, and, actually, when he realizes who Bud is, he softens completely.

14. What hit Bud as hard as Snaggletooth MacNevin had smacked Herman E. Calloway?
    "All of a sudden I knew that of all the places in the world that I'd ever been in this was the one. That of all the people I'd ever met these were the ones. This was where I was supposed to be." He knew he had found his real home.

15. Give two examples of Bud's practical nature and common sense in being able to fend for himself?
    Many answers would be correct. Use your own judgement.

16. What finally convinced Herman E. Calloway that Bud might be his relative? What was the final proof that Bud's mother and Herman's daughter were one and the same?
    Bud produced the stones that Herman Calloway had sent to Bud's mother, HEC's daughter. The final proof was the picture Bud had of his mother.

17. Why didn't Bud need his suitcase items anymore? What did he do with the flyers, stones, and picture of his mother?
    He realized they had served their useful purpose, and he didn't need them now that he was home. He gave the stones and flyers to Herman E. Calloway. He hung the picture of his mother on the wall in her (now his) room.

18. What did the squeaks and squawks of the saxophone sound like to Bud?
    They sounded like one door closing and another door opening.

III. REAL PEOPLE, PLACES & THINGS

Choose **five** of these people, places or things that Bud mentions in the book and identify them:

John Dillinger	Louisville Slugger	Baby Face Nelson	Last Supper
Paul Bunyan	Paul Robeson	J. Edgar Hoover	Pretty Boy Floyd
Herbert Hoover	Machine Gun Kelly	Al Capone	Organized Labor
Ku Klux Klan	Packard	John Brown	

IV. Vocabulary

Choose ten of the vocabulary words to dictate for students to write down for this section of the test.

ADVANCED SHORT ANSWER UNIT TEST - *Bud, Not Buddy*

I. Matching/Identify

_____ 1. Caldwell   A. Lefty's daughter

_____ 2. Todd Amos   B. Bud's grandfather's last name

_____ 3. Momma   C. gave Bud a ride to Grand Rapids

_____ 4. Calloway   D. looked unhappy in the picture at the Miss B. Gotten Moon Park

_____ 5. Bugs   E. shoved a pencil up Bud's nose

_____ 6. Clarence   F. left Hooverville on the train headed west

_____ 7. Deza   G. Bud's last name

_____ 8. Lefty   H. kissed Bud after washing dishes in Hooverville

_____ 9. Steady Eddie   I. Bud's pretend name

_____ 10. Miss Thomas   J. restaurant where the band went

_____ 11. Sweet Pea   K. gave Bud a new case

_____ 12. Mrs. Sleet   L. vocal stylist who took care of Bud

II. Short Answer

1. From what point of view is *Bud, Not Buddy* written? What advantages did using that point of view give the author?

2. List three people who helped Bud along his way and tell what each person did for him.

Bud, Not Buddy Advanced Short Answer Unit Test page 2

3. Give three examples of Bud's practical nature and common sense.

4. Give two examples of times that Bud's imagination added interest to the book.

5. Describe Momma. Take all the clues we get about her through the book and tell who she was.

6. What is the importance of each of the following: the suitcase(s), the flyers, the blanket, and the stones?

   Suitcase

   Flyer(s)

   Blanket

   Stones

Bud, Not Buddy Advanced Short Answer Unit Test Page 3

7. Name one character trait that Bud and his grandfather shared. Give an example of how each of them exhibited that trait at some point in the book.

8. What did the sign at the mission mean: "There's No Place Like America Today!"? What was it intended to mean, according to the pictures on the sign, and what did it mean to the people who saw it at the mission?

9. Give two examples of events Christopher Paul Curtis used in this book to make social commentary.

10. Momma told Bud no to worry, that when one door closes, another door opens. Cite and explain three times in the book where a door closed for Bud and another door opened.

Bud, Not Buddy Advanced Short Answer Unit Test page 4

III. Composition

    The book *Bud, Not Buddy* is a touching story of one boy's quest to find his place in the world. It is often humorous and is fun to read, but it also has several very serious and important messages that the author intends for us to understand. What is the most important message we should take away from our reading of this book? Explain what that message is, how it was developed in the book and why it is important for us to understand that message.

Bud, Not Buddy Advanced Short Answer Unit Test page 5

IV. Vocabulary

Listen to the vocabulary words and write them down. After you have written down all the words, write a paragraph using all of the vocabulary words. The paragraph must in some way relate to *Bud, Not Buddy*.

MULTIPLE CHOICE UNIT TEST 1 - *Bud, Not Buddy*

I. Matching/Identify

_____ 1. Caldwell A. looked unhappy in the picture at the Miss B. Gotten Moon Park

_____ 2. Todd Amos B. kissed Bud after washing dishes in Hooverville

_____ 3. Momma C. gave Bud a ride to Grand Rapids

_____ 4. Calloway D. Bud's last name

_____ 5. Bugs E. shoved a pencil up Bud's nose

_____ 6. Clarence F. gave Bud a new case

_____ 7. Deza G. Lefty's daughter

_____ 8. Lefty H. left Hooverville on the train headed west

_____ 9. Steady Eddie I. vocal stylist who took care of Bud

_____ 10. Miss Thomas J. Bud's grandfather's last name

_____ 11. Sweet Pea K. Bud's pretend name

_____ 12. Mrs. Sleet L. restaurant where the band went

II. Multiple Choice

1. What was printed on the blue flyer? Why was it special?
   A. The flyer was an advertisement for Herman E. Calloway and the Dusky Devastators of the Depression and a picture of a man standing next to a giant fiddle. Bud thought the man might be his father.
   B. The blue flyer had a picture of Bud's mother sitting on a horse at the Miss B. Gotten Moon Park. It was the only picture Bud had of his mother.
   C. The blue flyer had a list of the contents of Bud's suitcase so he could check to see that nothing was missing.
   D. The blue flyer was an advertisement for the mission where Bud sometimes ate. It was special because Bud needed the directions to the mission that were printed on it.

Bud, Not Buddy Multiple Choice Unit Test 1 Page 2

2. What was Bud's revenge plan against the Amoses?
   A. To throw the hornets' nest in their open bedroom window
   B. To shove a pencil up Todd's nose while he slept
   C. To remove the gun from the house and make Todd wet the bed
   D. To file a complaint about them at the orphanage/home

3. What did Bud's use of his blanket tell us about him?
   A. He was cold.
   B. He was smart, neat, and careful with his things.
   C. He was still really a baby.
   D. He had been injured escaping from the shed.

4. What did Momma tell Bud about his name?
   A. "Bud" was short for Budweiser, his father's favorite beer, which Bud had inadvertently taken a drink of when he was a toddler. It was a funny family incident that just stuck as a joke.
   B. Bud's real name was Beauregard, but folks called him "Bud" because it was shorter.
   C. Momma told Bud to "never mind about your name; it's "Bud" and that's it. Period."
   D. Momma chose "Bud" because he is like a flower blossom, full of love, waiting for the right warmth and care to open it up.

5. What did Momma tell Bud about doors?
   A. When one door closes, don't worry; another door opens.
   B. If you're scared of what's behind a door, just jam a chair under the knob and you'll be safe.
   C. Doors are just doors. Nothing to fear; nothing to anticipate.
   D. All of the above

6. What did Bud know about the library door's closing?
   A. It meant that he was stuck in the library, but at least would be safe, for the night.
   B. It meant he would be out on the street with no shelter for the night.
   C. It was the kind of door Momma had told him about. Since it had closed, another door was about to open.
   D. He knew that someone had closed the door, so he was not alone.

7. Why did Bud start wondering if going to California was the right thing to do?
   A. He was scared of traveling on the trains.
   B. He liked Deza and had new friends here he didn't want to leave.
   C. He knew people in Flint who could help him, but knew no one in California.
   D. He thought it was more likely he could find his own family closer to Flint.

8. Why did Bud miss the train from Hooverville?
   A. He went back to find Deza and say goodbye.
   B. The police held him back.
   C. He got stuck in a stampede of men and boys.
   D. He stopped to put his blue flyer in his pocket.

Bud, Not Buddy Multiple Choice Unit Test 1 Page 3

9. How are ideas like seeds?
    A. They start small and grow bigger than you ever thought they could.
    B. They don't take root unless you tend to them.
    C. They need a lot of weeding to keep the bad parts out.
    D. You have to dig a hole before they can really get started.

10. Why did Bud tell the man he had run away from Grand Rapids?
    A. He said it because it was true; he could not lie.
    B. He said that so the man would take him there.
    C. He said that just to tell him *something*; it didn't matter what.
    D. He said that thinking it would make the man leave him alone.

11. Why did Bud say that it's terrible to have been brought up proper?
    A. He couldn't not do the right thing.
    B. By having been brought up properly, he knew the good things that were missing in his life.
    C. Because of his proper upbringing, he didn't understand the way of life of the the people who had not been brought up properly.
    D. People who had not been brought up properly thought less of him because of his manners and nice ways. They were mean to him and teased him.

12. Why did Bud sleep so well in the car and through that first night with Mr. Lewis?
    A. He could finally relax because he was safe.
    B. He was with someone who cared about him.
    C. He was finally on his way to meet Herman E. Calloway.
    D. All of the above

13. What was Bud's reason for thinking it was okay to lie to an adult but not to a kid?
    A. Adults don't really care what you're saying as long as it accomplishes what they want in the end; kids really want to know.
    B. Adults are more used to lies than kids are.
    C. Adults actually expect kids to lie in certain circumstances; kids don't.
    D. It's more important what kids think of you than adults.

14. What warning did Herman E. Calloway give Bud about snooping around the house? What was Bud's reaction to Herman E. Calloway's warning?
    A. He warned Bud not to steal anything. Bud immediately wanted to steal something.
    B. He warned Bud not to steal anything. Bud was insulted and wanted to leave.
    C. He warned Bud not that if he went snooping around the house, he'd send him back to Flint.
    D. He warned Bud not to snoop around the house, that curiosity killed the cat.

Bud, Not Buddy Multiple Choice Unit Test 1 Page 4

15. What name did Bud get?
    A. They called him Sweet Pea.
    B. They called him Suitcase.
    C. They called him Sleepy LaBone
    D. They called him Stone Man

16. What finally convinced Herman E. Calloway that Bud might be his relative?
    A. The stones
    B. Bud's smile
    C. The way Bud talked
    D. Buds appreciation of music

17. What did Bud realize about the dead girl's room?
    A. It made Herman E. Calloway happy.
    B. It belonged to his mother.
    C. The closet connected to Mr. Calloway's room.
    D. It was kept better than the rest of the house.

18. What was written on the stones, and why was it written on them?
    A. Birth dates and birth places of Calloway relatives
    B. Books, chapters and verses from the Bible
    C. Dates and places Mr. Calloway's band had played
    D. Dates and places where Mr. Calloway took his daughter with the band

Bud, Not Buddy Multiple Choice Unit Test 1 Page 5

III. Quotations

1. "It was like something was telling me there was a message for me on this flyer but I didn't have the decoder ring to read what it was." What did the message on the flyer turn out to be?
    A. The message was that Bud would one day be a musician.
    B. The message was that Herman E. Calloway was Bud's grandfather, a band leader and performer in Grand Rapids.
    C. The message was that his mother was a vocalist for Herman Calloway's band.
    D. The message was that his grandfather kept changing the band's name so the FBI wouldn't be able to track him, since he was a labor organizer.

2. "I promise you suitcase will be safe here." I remembered the Amoses had promised the same thing." This quote was from Bud's Hooverville experiences. Compare/contrast how the Hoovervillians treated his suitcase with how the Amoses did.
    A. The Amoses gave his suitcase the respect it deserved; the Hoovervillians did not.
    B. The Hoovervillians gave his suitcase the respect it deserved; the Amoses did not.
    C. Neither the Amoses nor the Hoovervillians gave the suitcase the respect it deserved.
    D. Both the Amoses and the Hoovervillians gave the suitcase the respect it deserved.

3. "Maybe someone was trying to tell me something, what with me missing the train and the blue flyer floating back to me. . ." What was someone trying to tell Bud?
    A. He pays too much attention to detail.
    B. His life was always going to be full of bad luck.
    C. He should stay in Michigan and not go west.
    D. He will always be on his own.

4. "It's funny how ideas are, in a lot of ways they're just like seeds. Both of them start real, real small, and then . . . woop, zoop, sloop . . . before you can say Jack Robinson they've gone and grown a lot bigger than you ever thought they could." What was the idea that Bud was talking about here?
    A. The idea that he should go west
    B. The idea that he should stay in Michigan.
    C. The idea of his revenge plan for the Amoses
    D. The idea that Herman E. Calloway was his father

5. "I wonder how grown folks know so doggone much by just looking at you." To what was Bud referring when he thought this?
    A. He was referring to the fact that Lefty knew he was a hungry boy from Flint.
    B. He was referring to the fact that the Librarian knew he would attempt to go see Miss Hill.
    C. He was referring to the fact that the police officer at the mission knew he had run away from the Amoses and the home.
    D. He was referring to the fact that the Hoovervillians knew he would miss the train.

Bud, Not Buddy Short Answer Unit Test 1 Page 6

6. "Sometimes it's terrible to have been brought up proper." Why did Bud say this?
   A. He regretted having manners and not fitting in with the people at the mission.
   B. He regretted knowing the right thing to do because then he felt like he had to do it.
   C. He regretted being brought up proper because it made him long for all the finer things in life that he couldn't have now.
   D. He regretted knowing right from wrong and having to apologize for being wrong.

7. "We hadn't been driving for a minute before he started asking a whole slew of questions. Questions that I had to be very careful about giving the right answers to." What did this tell us about Bud?
   A. Bud couldn't tell a lie.
   B. Bud had to give answers that would be consistent with his lies.
   C. Bud was cautious but wanted to tell Lefty everything truthfully so Lefty could help him.
   D. Bud was "brought up proper;" he had to be totally truthful.

8. "Go ahead and cry, Bud, you're home." Who said this to Bud?
   A. Herman E. Calloway
   B. Mrs. Sleet
   C. Jimmy
   D. Miss Thomas

9. "Herman E. Calloway didn't have to worry, I was a liar, not a thief." What does this quote tell us about Bud?
   A. Bud didn't want to worry anyone.
   B. Bud knows himself pretty well.
   C. Bud doesn't understand Herman E. Calloway.
   D. Bud was compassionate.

10. "I took in a deep, deep breath and it felt like I was sleeping with my own blanket wrapped around my head. I took in a couple more deep breaths and I could hear Momma starting to read another story to me." Where was Bud? Why did he feel like he was sleeping with his own blanket around his head?
    A. He was under the Christmas tree. He did have his own blanket over his head.
    B. He was in the library, falling asleep on a book.
    C. He was in Hooverville, relieved to be with people who would look out for him.
    D. He was in his mother's room, at home.

Bud, Not Buddy Multiple Choice Unit Test 1 Page 7

IV. Vocabulary: Match the word to the definition

____ 1. TEMPORARY   A. Recognize something's value
____ 2. HOODLUM   B. Not permanent; just for a while
____ 3. MIDGET   C. Relative
____ 4. ILK   D. Thinking of what will benefit others
____ 5. INSISTED   E. Kind, group, set
____ 6. LUGGED   F. Valuable
____ 7. CONSIDERATE   G. Short pants
____ 8. TOLERATE   H. Small in size
____ 9. MISSION   I. Carried
____ 10. PRECIOUS   J. Mistreating; tormenting; abusing
____ 11. ESPECIALLY   K. Hotness or coldness
____ 12. TEMPERATURE   L. Small-time criminal
____ 13. RECOGNIZED   M. Repeatedly demanded
____ 14. FOSTER   N. Act of God; something impossible happens
____ 15. TORTURING   O. Particularly
____ 16. MATRIMONIAL   P. Attack or invasion, sometimes to uncover something illegal
____ 17. REPUTATION   Q. Having the effect of putting one in a trance or asleep
____ 18. MIRACLE   R. Identified
____ 19. CONCLUSIONS   S. A person's character observed by others
____ 20. KIN   T. Relating to marriage
____ 21. HYPNOTIZING   U. Results, decisions, deductions
____ 22. ALIAS   V. Charitable, usually religious, house for helping needy people
____ 23. KNICKERS   W. Temporary care
____ 24. APPRECIATE   X. Put up with; endure
____ 25. RAID   Y. A made-up name usually assumed to hide one's true identity

Bud, Not Buddy Multiple Choice Unit Test 1 Page 8

III. Composition

Usually when people are related, they have certain traits in common. Look at Bud, Momma and Herman E. Calloway and explain in what ways they are alike, how it is evident that they are from the same family.

MULTIPLE CHOICE UNIT TEST 2 - *Bud, Not Buddy*

I. Matching/Identify

_____ 1. Caldwell   A. Lefty's daughter

_____ 2. Todd Amos   B. Bud's grandfather's last name

_____ 3. Momma   C. gave Bud a ride to Grand Rapids

_____ 4. Calloway   D. looked unhappy in the picture at the Miss B. Gotten Moon Park

_____ 5. Bugs   E. shoved a pencil up Bud's nose

_____ 6. Clarence   F. left Hooverville on the train headed west

_____ 7. Deza   G. Bud's last name

_____ 8. Lefty   H. kissed Bud after washing dishes in Hooverville

_____ 9. Steady Eddie   I. Bud's pretend name

_____ 10. Miss Thomas   J. restaurant where the band went

_____ 11. Sweet Pea   K. gave Bud a new case

_____ 12. Mrs. Sleet   L. vocal stylist who took care of Bud

II. Multiple Choice

1. According to Bud, did he have a better foster family assignment than Jerry did? Explain. Was he right?
    A. Bud thought Jerry had the better assignment because the little girls would take good care of him. No, he wasn't right.
    B. Bud thought he had the better assignment because he had a boy to play with. Yes, he was right.
    C. Bud thought Jerry had the worse assignment because the girls would be fussy and want him to play girl-stuff, like dolls. Yes, he was right.
    D. Bud thought he had the worse assignment because the boy would want to fight with him. Yes, he was right.

2. Why did Bud get mad after he got out of the shed?
    A. He was mad at himself for getting into that situation.
    B. He was mad at the home for giving him such a terrible assignment.
    C. He was mad because he was alone and scared.
    D. He was mad at his mother for leaving him.

Bud, Not Buddy Multiple Choice Unit Test 2 Page 2

3. What did Bud's use of his blanket tell us about him? What did the blanket symbolize?
   A. It tells us he was still a baby, carrying a blanket around. It symbolized his immaturity.
   B. It tells us he was practical. It symbolized home and mother.
   C. It tells us he was cold. It didn't symbolize anything.
   D. It tells us he was creative. It symbolized his independence.

4. Why was Bud's name "Bud," not "Buddy"?
   A. "Buddy" was too childish for him; "Bud" was more adult.
   B. The boys at the home called him "Buddy," and he hated it.
   C. He was a flower bud waiting for the right conditions to bloom.
   D. It was symbolic of the fact that he didn't want to be anyone's friend, anyone's "buddy."

5. Why did the author include the part about Bud's pretend family at the mission?
   A. He used them only to show that there were other poor people in Michigan; Bud wasn't the only one who was homeless.
   B. He used them only to point out the sign "There's no place like America today!"
   C. This pretend family was symbolic of Bud's hopes and dreams being stripped away.
   D. Bud's interaction with the family pointed out again that being poor and homeless doesn't necessarily mean "bad." Sometimes poor and homeless people are more caring and moral than people who have lots of money.

6. The library and librarian(s) were a significant part of the book. How were they used?
   A. The library was a temporary, safe home. The librarians were "mother" figures who helped Bud.
   B. The library and librarians represented the government and it's desire to take care of us all.
   C. The library represented the knowledge of mankind, and the librarians were the guardians of the knowledge.
   D. The library and librarians were representative only of another part of society which was neither particularly good or particularly evil; just another part of an uncaring universe.

7. The white people with the sick baby at Hooverville were very minor characters but were significant. Why?
   A. They showed just how ignorant prejudice can be.
   B. The sick baby was symbolic of a sick society.
   C. They made the homeless people seem stupid.
   D. They were just like the rest of the Hoovervillians. Even though they were white, they mixed right in with and were at home with all the other poor people, regardless of color.

Bud, Not Buddy Multiple Choice Unit Test 2 Page 3

8. How did the blue flyer lead Bud to his real home?
    A. The giant fiddle pointed to Grand Rapids when the blue flyer floated out from under the suitcase string, so Bud figured he'd better go to Grand Rapids.
    B. The flyer gave him the idea that Herman E. Calloway was his father. The flyer's falling out of the suitcase string also caused him to miss the train west.
    C. Lefty had had the blue flyers printed in Flint. He recognized Bud's immediately and knew he needed to take Bud to Grand Rapids.
    D. All of the above

9. Why did Bud tell Lefty that he had run away from Grand Rapids? Did it work?
    A. He thought that since Lefty had just come from Grand Rapids, he wouldn't want to go back there, that he would just continue on his way and leave Bud alone. No, it didn't work.
    B. He told Lefty he had run away from Grand Rapids because he did. He wanted a ride to Flint, which Lefty gave him. Yes, it worked.
    C. He thought if he told Lefty he was from there, Lefty would want to take him "home," and he would get to the destination he wanted quicker. Yes, it worked.
    D. Bud told Lefty he had run away from the Amoses in Grand Rapids, that he had left the home, and a nice librarian there had shown him how to get to see his friend, Miss Hill, in Chicago.

10. Choose two examples of Bud's being smart and cautious.
    A. when he pretended to be asleep so he could eavesdrop more
    B. when he read the Civil War book
    C. when he told Lefty he was from Grand Rapids
    D. when he was in the Amos's shed

11. Choose two examples of how we know Momma was a good mother.
    A. Bud is polite and shows he has a conscience.
    B. She read to him and gave him advice.
    C. She left him a picture of herself at the Miss B. Gotten Moon Park and the blue flyer.
    D. She bought him a suitcase and a saxophone.

12. Why did Lefty tell Bud to come see him if he decided to travel again?
    A. His daughter really liked Bud and wanted him to stay with her and her children.
    B. He could get Bud discounted tickets on the train.
    C. He liked traveling with Bud and thought another trip with him would be fun.
    D. He didn't want Bud to get into any trouble.

13. What was Bud's first impression of Herman E. Calloway? Was it accurate?
    A. He thought HEC would be a wonderful father to have. No, it wasn't accurate.
    B. He thought HEC was going to be hard to get along with. Yes, it was accurate.
    C. He thought HEC was okay and would eventually have to love him. Yes, it was accurate.
    D. He thought HEC was a vampire. No, it wasn't accurate.

Bud, Not Buddy Multiple Choice Unit Test 2 Page 4

14. What hit Bud as hard as Snaggletooth MacNevin had smacked Herman E. Calloway?
    A. Herman E. Calloway's fist
    B. The band's music
    C. Herman E. Calloway's lack of a sense of humor
    D. The fact that he belonged there

15. What finally convinced Herman E. Calloway that Bud was be his relative?
    A. The stones and the picture
    B. The flyer and the stones
    C. Bud's musical ability
    D. A blood test

16. What did the squeaks and squawks of the saxophone sound like to Bud?
    A. Music
    B. Cacophony
    C. One door closing and another door opening
    D. The rhythm of his mother reading to him at night

Bud, Not Buddy Multiple Choice Unit Test 2 Page 5

III. REAL PEOPLE, PLACES & THINGS

Match.

_____ 1. John Dillinger   A. abolitionist; spoke against slavery

_____ 2. Louisville Slugger   B. 31st President of the United States

_____ 3. Baby Face Nelson   C. kidnapper, gangster who coined "g-man" phrase

_____ 4. Paul Bunyan   D. baseball bat

_____ 5. Paul Robeson   E. Public Enemy Number One betrayed by Lady In Red

_____ 6. J. Edgar Hoover   F. gangster who controlled Chicago's underworld

_____ 7. Herbert Hoover   G. illegal organization against equal rights; members wear white sheets or hooded robes to remain anonymous

_____ 8. Machine Gun Kelly   H. director of FBI for 48 years

_____ 9. Al Capone   I. legendary hero of lumber camps

_____ 10. Ku Klux Klan   J. Lester Gillis, part of Dillinger's gang

_____ 11. John Brown   K. American singer, actor, athlete & civil rights activist

Bud, Not Buddy Multiple Choice Unit Test 2 Page 6

IV. Vocabulary - Match the correct definitions to the words.

____ 1. MIRACLE   A. Easy to see
____ 2. PATIENT   B. Lightly or gently pushed
____ 3. HOODLUM   C. Results, decisions, deductions
____ 4. CONSIDERATE   D. Proper
____ 5. DELICIOUS   E. Relative
____ 6. RAID   F. Illness causing difficulty breathing
____ 7. MATRIMONIAL   G. Relating to marriage
____ 8. MISSION   H. Started; induced
____ 9. FUMBLING   I. Thinking of what will benefit others
____ 10. KIN   J. Able to wait
____ 11. CONCLUSIONS   K. Attack or invasion, sometimes to uncover something illegal
____ 12. VERMIN   L. Lecturing; reprimanding
____ 13. ASTHMA   M. Small-time criminal
____ 14. SUSPICIOUS   N. Wary, not trusting
____ 15. COPACETIC   O. Act of God; something impossible happens
____ 16. PRECIOUS   P. Mistreating; tormenting; abusing
____ 17. NUDGED   Q. Person who doesn't eat meat
____ 18. FIDGETING   R. Tastes good
____ 19. ILK   S. Nervously moving about or twitching
____ 20. APPRECIATE   T. Kind, group, set
____ 21. OBVIOUS   U. Valuable
____ 22. PROVOKED   V. Charitable, usually religious, house for helping needy people
____ 23. SCOLDING   W. Low life creatures like rats
____ 24. VEGETARIAN   X. Clumsily searching
____ 25. TORTURING   Y. Recognize something's value

ANSWER SHEET - *Bud, Not Buddy*
Multiple Choice Unit Test 1

I. Matching	II. Multiple Choice	III. Quotes	IV. Vocabulary
1. ___	1. ___	1. ___	1. ___
2. ___	2. ___	2. ___	2. ___
3. ___	3. ___	3. ___	3. ___
4. ___	4. ___	4. ___	4. ___
5. ___	5. ___	5. ___	5. ___
6. ___	6. ___	6. ___	6. ___
7. ___	7. ___	7. ___	7. ___
8. ___	8. ___	8. ___	8. ___
9. ___	9. ___	9. ___	9. ___
10. ___	10. ___	10. ___	10. ___
11. ___	11. ___		11. ___
12. ___	12. ___		12. ___
	13. ___		13. ___
	14. ___		14. ___
	15. ___		15. ___
	16.		16. ___
	17. ___		17. ___
	18. ___		18. ___
			19. ___
			20. ___
			21. ___
			22. ___
			23. ___
			24. ___
			25. ___

ANSWER SHEET - *Bud, Not Buddy*
Multiple Choice Unit Test 2

I. Matching	II. Multiple Choice	III. Real Things	IV. Vocabulary
1. ___	1. ___	1. ___	1. ___
2. ___	2. ___	2. ___	2. ___
3. ___	3. ___	3. ___	3. ___
4. ___	4. ___	4. ___	4. ___
5. ___	5. ___	5. ___	5. ___
6. ___	6. ___	6. ___	6. ___
7. ___	7. ___	7. ___	7. ___
8. ___	8. ___	8. ___	8. ___
9. ___	9. ___	9. ___	9. ___
10. ___	10. ___	10. ___	10. ___
11. ___	11. ___	11. ___	11. ___
12. ___	12. ___		12. ___
	13. ___		13. ___
	14. ___		14. ___
	15. ___		15. ___
	16.		16. ___
			17. ___
			18. ___
			19. ___
			20. ___
			21. ___
			22. ___
			23. ___
			24. ___
			25. ___

ANSWER KEY - *Bud, Not Buddy*
Multiple Choice Unit Tests

Answers to Unit Test 1 are in the left column. Answers to Unit Test 2 are in the right column.

I. Matching	II. Multiple Choice	III. Quotes/Real	IV. Vocabulary
1. D G	1. A D	1. B E	1. B O
2. E E	2. C A	2. B D	2. L J
3. A D	3. B B	3. C J	3. H M
4. J B	4. D C	4. D I	4. E I
5. H F	5. A D	5. A K	5. M R
6. K I	6. C A	6. B H	6. I K
7. B H	7. D A	7. B B	7. D G
8. C C	8. D B	8. D C	8. X V
9. F K	9. A C	9. B F	9. V X
10. I L	10. B A&C	10. D G	10. F E
11. L J	11. A A&B	11. A	11. O C
12. G A	12. D D		12. K W
	13. A B		13. R F
	14. A D		14. W N
	15. C A		15. J D
	16. A C		16. T U
	17. B		17. S B
	18. C		18. N S
			19. U T
			20. C Y
			21. Q A
			22. Y H
			23. G L
			24. A Q
			25. P P

UNIT RESOURCE MATERIALS

BULLETIN BOARD IDEAS - *Bud, Not Buddy*

1. Save one corner of the board for the best of students' *Bud, Not Buddy* writing assignments.

2. Take one of the word search puzzles from the extra activities and with a marker copy it over in a large size on the bulletin board. Write the clue words to find to one side. Invite students prior to and after class to find the words and circle them on the bulletin board.

3. Write several of the most significant quotations from the book onto the board on brightly colored paper.

4. Make a bulletin board listing the vocabulary words for this unit. As you complete sections of the novel and discuss the vocabulary for each section, write the definitions on the bulletin board. (If your board is one students face frequently, it will help them learn the words.)

5. Place a map of Michigan on the board for use as reference.

6. Plot Bud's travels on the bulletin board, making a time line/story plot line graphic.

7. Title the board THERE'S NO PLACE LIKE AMERICA TODAY. Have students bring in pictures they think represent that statement. Post them with some of the students' writing assignments relevant to that heading..

8. Divide the board into 5 sections: NAMES, RULES, DOORS, SUITCASES, & WRITING. Make it part of each group's assignment to create its section of the bulletin board.

9. Make a travel bulletin board about Michigan. See your local travel agent for pictures, brochures, etc.

10. Title the board Bud, Not Buddy: HELPING THE HOMELESS. Post information about agencies and ways people are trying to help those who are in need.

EXTRA ACTIVITIES

One of the difficulties in teaching a novel is that all students don't read at the same speed. One student who likes to read may take the book home and finish it in a day or two. Sometimes a few students finish the in-class assignments early. The problem, then, is finding suitable extra activities for students.

One thing that helps is to keep a little library in the classroom. For this unit on *Bud, Not Buddy*, you might check out from the school library other related books and articles about foster homes for orphaned children, sources of help for abused children, music in the big band era, mission kitchens and other places who feed the homeless, sources of help for homeless people, vampires and vampire stories, trains and travel by train, Michigan, mileage between cities, the instruments mentioned in the book, the KKK, gangs and gangsters, the FBI, movies and movie stars of the era, Christopher Paul Curtis, articles of criticism about *Bud, Not Buddy,* or other books by Christopher Paul Curtis.

Other things you may keep on hand are puzzles. We have made some relating directly to *Bud, Not Buddy* for you. Feel free to duplicate them.

Some students may like to draw. You might devise a contest or allow some extra-credit grade for students who draw characters or scenes from *Bud, Not Buddy*. Note, too, that if the students do not want to keep their drawings you may pick up some extra bulletin board materials this way. If you have a contest and you supply the prize (a CD, pizza, or something like that perhaps), you could, possibly, make the drawing itself a non-returnable entry fee (a good way to accumulate more bulletin board materials for future years).

The pages which follow contain games, puzzles and worksheets. The keys, when appropriate, immediately follow the puzzle or worksheet. There are two main groups of activities: one group for the unit; that is, generally relating to *Bud, Not Buddy* text, and another group of activities related strictly to *Bud, Not Buddy* vocabulary.

Directions for these games, puzzles and worksheets are self-explanatory. The object here is to provide you with extra materials you may use in any way you choose.

MORE ACTIVITIES - *Bud, Not Buddy*

1. Pick a chapter or scene with a great deal of dialogue and have the students act it out on a stage. (Perhaps you could assign various scenes to different groups of students so more than one scene could be acted and more students could participate.)

2. Have students design a book cover (front and back and inside flaps) for *Bud, Not Buddy*.

3. Have students design a bulletin board (ready to be put up; not just sketched) for *Bud, Not Buddy*.

4. Use some of the related topics mentioned earlier for an in-class library as topics for guest speakers.

5. Have students make a diary for Bud with one entry for each major event in the story.

6. Have your students discuss (and implement when possible) ways that people can help feed the hungry or help the homeless in their own communities and in the world.

7. Let students discuss or write about their own names and/or nicknames–what the name means, whether or not they like the name, how they got the nickname, etc.

8. Have a Bud, Not Buddy Day. Assign each student to be one character in the book, to come to class that day dressed as that character and to talk and act like that character. Play big band music and discuss the book. You could set up situations for characters to act out. Have Mrs. Sleet meet Herman E. Calloway. Have Bud meet Miss Hill on her return visit to Flint or Grand Rapids. Have Deza meet Steady Eddie. And so on.

WORD SEARCH - *Bud, Not Buddy*

All words in this list are associated with *Bud, Not Buddy*. The words are placed backwards, forward, diagonally, up and down. The included words are listed below the word search.

```
L A M S L E E T R A P I D S J F Z R C N
E H A A T W J O E U B Y E E Z E L A E Z
F O R X N J B G H F L T A G Z Y R I K D
T M G O A A H F T T B E D W J A T R N V
Y E E P L Z E I A B U D S N I A R T Y T
R D L H K F R D F C G N P D M E X R C V
Y O E O A I B D D A S Z O A M P A C M P
G O T N M S E L N P E M C E Y R L L I H
Z R D E O H R E A O N W O R B Y T A S V
H M A P S T T X R N O Z H I L R L R S F
G D F C J E H G G E T S L L E E G E I M
Z O O P E A O G K F S J E V G Y E N O N
E D D I E R M O O N F K O N C D B C N V
B L O O D S A D U F X O A N S L E E P Y
M O M M A P S G W T H E R M A N Z R M X
```

AMOS	DEZA	HERMAN	MISSION	SLEEPY
ANGELA	DOOR	HOME	MOMMA	SLEET
BLOOD	EDDIE	HOOVER	MOON	STONES
BROWN	FBI	JERRY	PEA	TEARS
BUD	FIDDLE	JIMMY	RAPIDS	TELEGRAM
BUGS	FISH	KELLY	READ	THOMAS
CAPONE	FLINT	KLAN	RED	TRAIN
CAR	GRACE	LABOR	RULES	ZOOP
CLARENCE	GRANDFATHER	LAM	SAXOPHONE	
COPS	GUN	LEFTY	SEEDS	
DEAD	HERBERT	LIBRARY	SHED	

KEY: WORD SEARCH - *Bud, Not Buddy*

All words in this list are associated with *Bud, Not Buddy*. The words are placed backwards, forward, diagonally, up and down. The included words are listed below the word search.

```
L A M S L E E T R A P I D S J F   R C
E H A A       O E U B   E E     E L A E
F O R X N   B   H F L   A   Z   R I   D
T M G O A A H F T   B E D   J A   R N
Y E E P L   E I A B U D S N I A R T Y T
  D L H K F R D F C G   P D M E   R
  O E O A I B D D A S   O A M P A C M
G O T N M S E L N P E   C E Y R   L I
  R   E O H R E A O N W O R B Y   A S
    A   S T T   R N O     I L R L R S
      C   E H   G E T   L L E E   E I
Z O O P E A O       S   E V G   E N O
E D D I E R M O O N   K O N   D   C N
B L O O D S A   U     O A   S L E E P Y
M O M M A   S G     H E R M A N
```

AMOS	DEZA	HERMAN	MISSION	SLEEPY
ANGELA	DOOR	HOME	MOMMA	SLEET
BLOOD	EDDIE	HOOVER	MOON	STONES
BROWN	FBI	JERRY	PEA	TEARS
BUD	FIDDLE	JIMMY	RAPIDS	TELEGRAM
BUGS	FISH	KELLY	READ	THOMAS
CAPONE	FLINT	KLAN	RED	TRAIN
CAR	GRACE	LABOR	RULES	ZOOP
CLARENCE	GRANDFATHER	LAM	SAXOPHONE	
COPS	GUN	LEFTY	SEEDS	
DEAD	HERBERT	LIBRARY	SHED	

CROSSWORD *Bud, Not Buddy*

CROSSWORD CLUES - *Bud, Not Buddy*

ACROSS

1 It held Bud's blanket, flyer & things
4 Bud tried to drive Lefty's away
7 Miss Malone
9 ___, Not Buddy
11 On the ___; running away
12 Steady ___
13 Sweet ___; restaurant
14 Bud's had all dried up; he didn't cry often
18 ___ Janet; Momma
20 Ideas are a lot like these
22 ___ caps; men who handled baggage at the train
23 State where Bud lived
28 Guards at the shed door
29 Miss B. Gotten ___ Park
30 Place where Bud got food
31 Federal Bureau of Investigation
32 Horn player who helped Bud
33 Gone = ___ (Rule 28)

DOWN

2 Bud's last name
3 Mrs. ___ was Lefty's daughter
4 Herman E. ___
5. ___ & Things Number 328
6 Bud's word for the orphanage
7 When one closes, another one opens
8 They tried to keep the men off of the train
9 When wrapped in it, Bud felt close to Momma
10 HEC & The Dusky Devastators of the ___
15 Mr. ___ locked Bud in the shed
16 Had numbers & letters written on them
17 They had printed information about HEC and the band
19 1st part of the revenge plan was to get rid of this
20 Where Amoses locked Bud
21 A cockroach crawled in his ear
24 Mr. Calloway's first name
25 She was unhappy at the Miss B. Gotten Moon Park
26 Lefty was transporting this, so Bud thought he was a vampire
27 Mr. Lewis
28 City where Bud and Momma lived

CROSSWORD ANSWER KEY *Bud, Not Buddy*

MATCHING QUIZ/WORKSHEET 1 - *Bud, Not Buddy*

___ 1. BLOOD   A. ____ & Things Number 328

___ 2. ANGELA   B. Bud's word for the orphanage

___ 3. HOME   C. HEC's instrument; a giant ____

___ 4. MISSION   D. Miss Malone

___ 5. SLEEPY   E. Sweet ___; restaurant

___ 6. HOOVERVILLE   F. Miss Thomas's first name

___ 7. PEA   G. Mr. Calloway's first name

___ 8. HERMAN   H. State where Bud lived

___ 9. LEFTY   I. Al ____; leader of Chicago underworld

___ 10. MICHIGAN   J. They had printed information about HEC and the band

___ 11. GRACE   K. ___ caps; men who handled baggage at the train

___ 12. SHED   L. Place where Bud got food

___ 13. HORNETS   M. Where Amoses locked Bud

___ 14. CALLOWAY   N. J. Edgar ____; head of FBI for 48 years

___ 15. DEZA   O. Lefty was transporting this, so Bud thought he was a vampire

___ 16. SAXOPHONE   P. Instrument band gave to Bud

___ 17. HOOVER   Q. They tried to keep the men off of the train

___ 18. BLANKET   R. Cardboard town for the homeless

___ 19. RED   S. Mr. Lewis

___ 20. COPS   T. ___ LaBone; Bud

___ 21. RULES   U. ____ Janet; Momma

___ 22. FIDDLE   V. The vampire bat was actually this kind of a nest

___ 23. FLYERS   W. When wrapped in it, Bud felt close to Momma

___ 24. RAPIDS   X. Herman E. _____

___ 25. CAPONE   Y. Grand ____; where HEC lived

KEY: MATCHING QUIZ/WORKSHEET 1 - *Bud, Not Buddy*

O	1. BLOOD	A.	_____ & Things Number 328
U	2. ANGELA	B.	Bud's word for the orphanage
B	3. HOME	C.	HEC's instrument; a giant ____
L	4. MISSION	D.	Miss Malone
T	5. SLEEPY	E.	Sweet ___; restaurant
R	6. HOOVERVILLE	F.	Miss Thomas's first name
E	7. PEA	G.	Mr. Calloway's first name
G	8. HERMAN	H.	State where Bud lived
S	9. LEFTY	I.	Al ____; leader of Chicago underworld
H	10. MICHIGAN	J.	They had printed information about HEC and the band
F	11. GRACE	K.	___ caps; men who handled baggage at the train
M	12. SHED	L.	Place where Bud got food
V	13. HORNETS	M.	Where Amoses locked Bud
X	14. CALLOWAY	N.	J. Edgar ____; head of FBI for 48 years
D	15. DEZA	O.	Lefty was transporting this, so Bud thought he was a vampire
P	16. SAXOPHONE	P.	Instrument band gave to Bud
N	17. HOOVER	Q.	They tried to keep the men off of the train
W	18. BLANKET	R.	Cardboard town for the homeless
K	19. RED	S.	Mr. Lewis
Q	20. COPS	T.	___ LaBone; Bud
A	21. RULES	U.	____ Janet; Momma
C	22. FIDDLE	V.	The vampire bat was actually this kind of a nest
J	23. FLYERS	W.	When wrapped in it, Bud felt close to Momma
Y	24. RAPIDS	X.	Herman E. _____
I	25. CAPONE	Y.	Grand ____; where HEC lived

MATCHING QUIZ/WORKSHEET 2 - *Bud, Not Buddy*

____ 1. SLEET   A. Mr. ____ locked Bud in the shed

____ 2. HERMAN   B. ____ Hoover; President of United States

____ 3. RULES   C. Herman E. _____

____ 4. ANGELA   D. Gone = ____ (Rule 28)

____ 5. STATION   E. Mr. Calloway's first name

____ 6. FISH   F. They had printed information about HEC and the band

____ 7. ZOOP   G. ____ & Things Number 328

____ 8. GUN   H. Guards at the shed door

____ 9. CLARENCE   I. 1st part of the revenge plan was to get rid of this

____ 10. COPS   J. Miss ____; vocal stylist who took care of Bud

____ 11. BLOOD   K. John ____; abolitionist

____ 12. DEAD   L. Bud's pretend name at the mission

____ 13. FLYERS   M. They tried to keep the men off of the train

____ 14. BUGS   N. A cockroach crawled in his ear

____ 15. CALLOWAY   O. Lefty was transporting this, so Bud thought he was a vampire

____ 16. HERBERT   P. Mrs. ____ was Lefty's daughter

____ 17. TRAIN   Q. It held Bud's blanket, flyer & things

____ 18. MICHIGAN   R. Ku Klux ____; organization against equal rights; members anonymous

____ 19. RAPIDS   S. State where Bud lived

____ 20. SUITCASE   T. Grand Calloway _____

____ 21. AMOS   U. ____ Janet; Momma

____ 22. KLAN   V. Bud tried to drive Lefty's away

____ 23. BROWN   W. Grand ____; where HEC lived

____ 24. CAR   X. The boys wanted to hop on one going west

____ 25. THOMAS   Y. Whoop, ____, Sloop!

KEY: MATCHING QUIZ/WORKSHEET 2 - *Bud, Not Buddy*

P	1. SLEET	A. Mr. ___ locked Bud in the shed
E	2. HERMAN	B. ___ Hoover; President of United States
G	3. RULES	C. Herman E. ___
U	4. ANGELA	D. Gone = ___ (Rule 28)
T	5. STATION	E. Mr. Calloway's first name
H	6. FISH	F. They had printed information about HEC and the band
Y	7. ZOOP	G. ___ & Things Number 328
I	8. GUN	H. Guards at the shed door
L	9. CLARENCE	I. 1st part of the revenge plan was to get rid of this
M	10. COPS	J. Miss ___; vocal stylist who took care of Bud
O	11. BLOOD	K. John ___; abolitionist
D	12. DEAD	L. Bud's pretend name at the mission
F	13. FLYERS	M. They tried to keep the men off of the train
N	14. BUGS	N. A cockroach crawled in his ear
C	15. CALLOWAY	O. Lefty was transporting this, so Bud thought he was a vampire
B	16. HERBERT	P. Mrs. ___ was Lefty's daughter
X	17. TRAIN	Q. It held Bud's blanket, flyer & things
S	18. MICHIGAN	R. Ku Klux ___; organization against equal rights; members anonymous
W	19. RAPIDS	S. State where Bud lived
Q	20. SUITCASE	T. Grand Calloway ___
A	21. AMOS	U. ___ Janet; Momma
R	22. KLAN	V. Bud tried to drive Lefty's away
K	23. BROWN	W. Grand ___; where HEC lived
V	24. CAR	X. The boys wanted to hop on one going west
J	25. THOMAS	Y. Whoop, ___, Sloop!

JUGGLE LETTER 1 - Bud, Not Buddy

1. UNG = 1. _____
   1st part of the revenge plan was to get rid of this

2. IFB = 2. _____
   Federal Bureau of Investigation

3. EABLTKN = 3. _____
   When wrapped in it, Bud felt close to Momma

4. RTRBHEE = 4. _____
   ____ Hoover; President of United States

5. ILABRRY = 5. _____
   Bud looked for Miss Hill there

6. TLFNI = 6. _____
   City where Bud & Momma lived

7. EDDLFI = 7. _____
   HEC's instrument; a giant ____

8. RMAEHN = 8. _____
   Mr. Calloway's first name

9. DOBLO = 9. _____
   Lefty was transporting this, so Bud thought he was a vampire

10. SSDEE =10. _____
    Ideas are a lot like these

11. EDAZ =11. _____
    Miss Malone

12. RIANT =12. _____
    The boys wanted to hop on one going west

13. ATTNIOS =13. _____
    Grand Calloway _____

14. AENSPHOOX =14. _____
    Instrument band gave to Bud

15. RALOB =15. _____
    Police stopped Lefty looking for ___ organizers

16. ALLLWCED	=16. _____	
	Bud's last name	
17. OPZO	=17. _____	
	Whoop, _____, Sloop!	
18. GELAAN	=18. _____	
	_____ Janet; Momma	
19. RTRDEHFANAG	=19. _____	
	HEC to Bud	
20. NALK	=20. _____	
	Ku Klux _____; organization against equal rights; members anonymous	
21. DER	=21. _____	
	_____ caps; men who handled baggage at the train	
22. AEP	=22. _____	
	Sweet _____; restaurant	
23. STOMHA	=23. _____	
	Miss _____; vocal stylist who took care of Bud	
24. ASERT	=24. _____	
	Bud's had all dried up; he didn't cry often	
25. UDB	=25. _____	
	_____, Not Buddy	
26. OREVHO	=26. _____	
	J. Edgar _____; head of FBI for 48 years	
27. MAL	=27. _____	
	On the _____; running away	
28. MMIJY	=28. _____	
	Horn player who helped Bud	
29. GTEEAMLR	=29. _____	
	Lefty sent one to HEC, advising him of Bud's whereabouts	
30. EERNSODIPS	=30. _____	
	HEC & The Dusky Devastators of the _____	
31. RVOOELLEIVH	=31. _____	
	Cardboard town for the homeless	

JUGGLE LETTER 1 ANSWER KEY - Bud, Not Buddy

1. UNG = 1. GUN
   1st part of the revenge plan was to get rid of this

2. IFB = 2. FBI
   Federal Bureau of Investigation

3. EABLTKN = 3. BLANKET
   When wrapped in it, Bud felt close to Momma

4. RTRBHEE = 4. HERBERT
   ____ Hoover; President of United States

5. ILABRRY = 5. LIBRARY
   Bud looked for Miss Hill there

6. TLFNI = 6. FLINT
   City where Bud & Momma lived

7. EDDLFI = 7. FIDDLE
   HEC's instrument; a giant ____

8. RMAEHN = 8. HERMAN
   Mr. Calloway's first name

9. DOBLO = 9. BLOOD
   Lefty was transporting this, so Bud thought he was a vampire

10. SSDEE = 10. SEEDS
    Ideas are a lot like these

11. EDAZ = 11. DEZA
    Miss Malone

12. RIANT = 12. TRAIN
    The boys wanted to hop on one going west

13. ATTNIOS = 13. STATION
    Grand Calloway ____

14. AENSPHOOX = 14. SAXOPHONE
    Instrument band gave to Bud

15. RALOB = 15. LABOR
    Police stopped Lefty looking for ___ organizers

16. ALLLWCED = 16. CALDWELL
Bud's last name

17. OPZO = 17. ZOOP
Whoop, ____, Sloop!

18. GELAAN = 18. ANGELA
____ Janet; Momma

19. RTRDEHFANAG = 19. GRANDFATHER
HEC to Bud

20. NALK = 20. KLAN
Ku Klux ____; organization against equal rights; members anonymous

21. DER = 21. RED
____ caps; men who handled baggage at the train

22. AEP = 22. PEA
Sweet ____; restaurant

23. STOMHA = 23. THOMAS
Miss ____; vocal stylist who took care of Bud

24. ASERT = 24. TEARS
Bud's had all dried up; he didn't cry often

25. UDB = 25. BUD
____, Not Buddy

26. OREVHO = 26. HOOVER
J. Edgar ____; head of FBI for 48 years

27. MAL = 27. LAM
On the ____; running away

28. MMIJY = 28. JIMMY
Horn player who helped Bud

29. GTEEAMLR = 29. TELEGRAM
Lefty sent one to HEC, advising him of Bud's whereabouts

30. EERNSODIPS = 30. DEPRESSION
HEC & The Dusky Devastators of the _____

31. RVOOELLEIVH = 31. HOOVERVILLE
Cardboard town for the homeless

JUGGLE LETTER 2 - Bud, Not Buddy

1. EEDDI = 1. _____
   Steady ____

2. STSONE = 2. _____
   Had numbers & letters written on them

3. PSOC = 3. _____
   They tried to keep the men off of the train

4. GSUB = 4. _____
   A cockroach crawled in his ear

5. IFSH = 5. _____
   Guards at the shed door

6. WOBRN = 6. _____
   John ____; abolitionist

7. MHEO = 7. _____
   Bud's word for the orphanage

8. IMSSONI = 8. _____
   Place where Bud got food

9. DESH = 9. _____
   Where Amoses locked Bud

10. NLAECCER =10. _____
    Bud's pretend name at the mission

11. YTLFE =11. _____
    Mr. Lewis

12. RLFEYS =12. _____
    They had printed information about HEC and the band

13. AEUICSST =13. _____
    It held Bud's blanket, flyer & things

14. MAMMO =14. _____
    She was unhappy at the Miss B. Gotten Moon Park

15. LEKYL =15. _____
    Machine Gun ____; gangster

16. JEYRR =16. _____
He got a foster home with girls

17. YEPLSE =17. _____
___ LaBone; Bud

18. YCWLALAO =18. _____
Herman E. _____

19. OORD =19. _____
When one closes, another one opens

20. PCOANE =20. _____
Al ____; leader of Chicago underworld

21. ERAD =21. _____
Momma ___ to Bud until he fell asleep

22. AMCHINGI =22. _____
State where Bud lived

23. EURLS =23. _____
_____ & Things Number 328

24. ESTLE =24. _____
Mrs. ___ was Lefty's daughter

25. ARC =25. _____
Bud tried to drive Lefty's away

26. DDAE =26. _____
Gone = ____ (Rule 28)

27. ARPSID =27. _____
Grand ____; where HEC lived

28. ERCAG =28. _____
Miss Thomas's first name

29. OMON =29. _____
Miss B. Gotten ____ Park

30. SMAO =30. _____
Mr. ___ locked Bud in the shed

31. SRHETON =31. _____
The vampire bat was actually this kind of a nest

JUGGLE LETTER 2 ANSWER KEY - Bud, Not Buddy

1. EEDDI = 1. EDDIE
Steady ____

2. STSONE = 2. STONES
Had numbers & letters written on them

3. PSOC = 3. COPS
They tried to keep the men off of the train

4. GSUB = 4. BUGS
A cockroach crawled in his ear

5. IFSH = 5. FISH
Guards at the shed door

6. WOBRN = 6. BROWN
John ____; abolitionist

7. MHEO = 7. HOME
Bud's word for the orphanage

8. IMSSONI = 8. MISSION
Place where Bud got food

9. DESII = 9. SHED
Where Amoses locked Bud

10. NLAECCER =10. CLARENCE
Bud's pretend name at the mission

11. YTLFE =11. LEFTY
Mr. Lewis

12. RLFEYS =12. FLYERS
They had printed information about HEC and the band

13. AEUICSST =13. SUITCASE
It held Bud's blanket, flyer & things

14. MAMMO =14. MOMMA
She was unhappy at the Miss B. Gotten Moon Park

15. LEKYL =15. KELLY
Machine Gun ____; gangster

16. JEYRR =16. JERRY
He got a foster home with girls

17. YEPLSE =17. SLEEPY
___ LaBone; Bud

18. YCWLALAO =18. CALLOWAY
Herman E. _____

19. OORD =19. DOOR
When one closes, another one opens

20. PCOANE =20. CAPONE
Al ____; leader of Chicago underworld

21. ERAD =21. READ
Momma ___ to Bud until he fell asleep

22. AMCHINGI =22. MICHIGAN
State where Bud lived

23. EURLS =23. RULES
_____ & Things Number 328

24. ESTLE =24. SLEET
Mrs. ___ was Lefty's daughter

25. ARC =25. CAR
Bud tried to drive Lefty's away

26. DDAE =26. DEAD
Gone = ____ (Rule 28)

27. ARPSID =27. RAPIDS
Grand ____; where HEC lived

28. ERCAG =28. GRACE
Miss Thomas's first name

29. OMON =29. MOON
Miss B. Gotten ____ Park

30. SMAO =30. AMOS
Mr. ___ locked Bud in the shed

31. SRHETON =31. HORNETS
The vampire bat was actually this kind of a nest

WORD LIST Bud, Not Buddy

No.	Word	Clue/Definition
1.	AMOS	Mr. ___ locked Bud in the shed
2.	ANGELA	___ Janet; Momma
3.	BLANKET	When wrapped in it, Bud felt close to Momma
4.	BLOOD	Lefty was transporting this, so Bud thought he was a vampire
5.	BROWN	John ___; abolitionist
6.	BUD	___, Not Buddy
7.	BUGS	A cockroach crawled in his ear
8.	CALDWELL	Bud's last name
9.	CALLOWAY	Herman E. _____
10.	CAPONE	Al ___; leader of Chicago underworld
11.	CAR	Bud tried to drive Lefty's away
12.	CLARENCE	Bud's pretend name at the mission
13.	COPS	They tried to keep the men off of the train
14.	DEAD	Gone = ___ (Rule 28)
15.	DEPRESSION	HEC & The Dusky Devastators of the _____
16.	DEZA	Miss Malone
17.	DOOR	When one closes, another one opens
18.	EDDIE	Steady ___
19.	FBI	Federal Bureau of Investigation
20.	FIDDLE	HEC's instrument; a giant ___
21.	FISH	Guards at the shed door
22.	FLINT	City where Bud & Momma lived
23.	FLYERS	They had printed information about HEC and the band
24.	GRACE	Miss Thomas's first name
25.	GRANDFATHER	HEC to Bud
26.	GUN	1st part of the revenge plan was to get rid of this
27.	HERBERT	___ Hoover; President of United States
28.	HERMAN	Mr. Calloway's first name
29.	HOME	Bud's word for the orphanage
30.	HOOVER	J. Edgar ___; head of FBI for 48 years
31.	HOOVERVILLE	Cardboard town for the homeless
32.	HORNETS	The vampire bat was actually this kind of a nest
33.	JERRY	He got a foster home with girls
34.	JIMMY	Horn player who helped Bud
35.	KELLY	Machine Gun ___; gangster
36.	KLAN	Ku Klux ___; organization against equal rights; members anonymous
37.	LABOR	Police stopped Lefty looking for ___ organizers
38.	LAM	On the ___; running away
39.	LEFTY	Mr. Lewis
40.	LIBRARY	Bud looked for Miss Hill there
41.	MICHIGAN	State where Bud lived
42.	MISSION	Place where Bud got food
43.	MOMMA	She was unhappy at the Miss B. Gotten Moon Park
44.	MOON	Miss B. Gotten ___ Park
45.	PEA	Sweet ___; restaurant
46.	RAPIDS	Grand ___; where HEC lived
47.	READ	Momma ___ to Bud until he fell asleep
48.	RED	___ caps; men who handled baggage at the train

WORD LIST Bud, Not Buddy continued

No. Word	Clue/Definition
49. RULES	_____ & Things Number 328
50. SAXOPHONE	Instrument band gave to Bud
51. SEEDS	Ideas are a lot like these
52. SHED	Where Amoses locked Bud
53. SLEEPY	___ LaBone; Bud
54. SLEET	Mrs. ___ was Lefty's daughter
55. STATION	Grand Calloway _____
56. STONES	Had numbers & letters written on them
57. SUITCASE	It held Bud's blanket, flyer & things
58. TEARS	Bud's had all dried up; he didn't cry often
59. TELEGRAM	Lefty sent one to HEC, advising him of Bud's whereabouts
60. THOMAS	Miss ___; vocal stylist who took care of Bud
61. TRAIN	The boys wanted to hop on one going west
62. ZOOP	Whoop, _____, Sloop!

VOCABULARY RESOURCE MATERIALS

VOCABULARY WORD SEARCH - *Bud, Not Buddy*

```
O B V I O U S S C I N S I S T E D A S T H M A A K
C W F N W F K C O L N N A E S O X K T D M I L P Q
G C M Z F S T O N K I G G C M V R N S J G R I P F
H O O D L U M L C T K D R I R R E T S O F A A R D
Y P L E Z O D D E E I B S A Y I E G U V K C S E X
P A R V J I C I R M H S Z N T D F C E R Q L X C V
N C S O B C G N N P I F O A S I R I O T I E B I D
O E N U V E V G S O X I P E O A T A C G A N M A G
T T O R G R W K N R T D K R S R V U D E N R G T Z
I I I E R P D R M A K G N M O P H E D I F I I E Y
Z C S D R E N U T R C E I X A V E R R E A K Z A W
I X U M D C L U N Y R T C D C T O C C M V T W E N
N B L I Q G P J G Y L I K P E C R K I Q I J I E D
G W C R C E T N Z N U N E P C L G I E A T N T N Q
C E N M R T I N T U G G R L F C I B M D L A Z G G
D Q O W Y L V Z R D G N S K V C X C Y O R L F H J
B J C W B P B L Z G E S F S J Y L P I E N G Y X P
N D M M T E T A R E D I S N O C S R L O Y I X W M
C B U G J W P B T D S U S P I C I O U S U V A F V
L F G D L D F C M T E M P E R A T U R E L S H L C
```

ALIAS	ESPECIALLY	KIN	PATIENT	TEMPERATURE
APPRECIATE	FIDGETING	KNICKERS	PRECIOUS	TEMPORARY
ASTHMA	FOSTER	LUGGED	PROVOKED	TOLERATE
CONCERN	FUMBLING	MATRIMONIAL	RADIATING	TORTURING
CONCLUSIONS	GLUM	MIDGET	RAID	VEGETARIAN
CONSIDERATE	HOODLUM	MIRACLE	RECOGNIZED	VERMIN
COPACETIC	HYPNOTIZING	MISSION	REPUTATION	
DECIDED	ILK	NUDGED	SACRIFICE	
DELICIOUS	INGRATITUDE	OBVIOUS	SCOLDING	
DEVOURED	INSISTED	ORNERY	SUSPICIOUS	

VOCABULARY WORD SEARCH ANSWER KEY
Bud, Not Buddy

```
              O B V I O U S S C I N S I S T E D A S T H M A A
                    C O L N   A E   O       T       I L P
          C       S   O N K I G G C M V R N         R I P
        H O O D L U M L C T K D R I R R E T S O F A A R
        Y P   E   O   D E E I   S A   I E G U     C S E
        P A   V   I   I R M   S   N T D F C E R   L   C
        N C S O   C   N N P I F O A   I R I O T I E   I
        O E N U   E   G   O   I P E O A T A C G A N   A
        T T O R   R     N R T D K R S R V U D E N R G T
        I I I E   P D   M A   G N M O P   E D I   I I E
        Z C S D   E   U T R   E I   A V E   R E A   Z A
        I   U   D   L U   Y R T C D   T O C   M   T   E N
        N   L I   G P   G Y L I K   E   R K I   I E D
        G   C   E   N   N U N E     L   I E A   N T N
          E N   R I     U G G R       I   M D L A     G
        D   O     L     D G S         C   O R L
              C   B     G E               I E N   Y
                M   E T A R E D I S N O C     L O   I
                U             D S U S P I C I O U S U   A
              F               T E M P E R A T U R E   S   L
```

ALIAS	ESPECIALLY	KIN	PATIENT	TEMPERATURE
APPRECIATE	FIDGETING	KNICKERS	PRECIOUS	TEMPORARY
ASTHMA	FOSTER	LUGGED	PROVOKED	TOLERATE
CONCERN	FUMBLING	MATRIMONIAL	RADIATING	TORTURING
CONCLUSIONS	GLUM	MIDGET	RAID	VEGETARIAN
CONSIDERATE	HOODLUM	MIRACLE	RECOGNIZED	VERMIN
COPACETIC	HYPNOTIZING	MISSION	REPUTATION	
DECIDED	ILK	NUDGED	SACRIFICE	
DELICIOUS	INGRATITUDE	OBVIOUS	SCOLDING	
DEVOURED	INSISTED	ORNERY	SUSPICIOUS	

VOCABULARY CROSSWORD *Bud, Not Buddy*

VOCABULARY CROSSWORD CLUES - *Bud, Not Buddy*

ACROSS
1 Clumsily searching
3 Mistreating; tormenting; abusing
8 Not permanent; just for a while
10 A made-up name usually assumed to hide one's true identity
11 Chose
12 Kind, group, set
13 Hotness or coldness
15 Low life creatures like rats
17 Sad
20 Repeatedly demanded
22 Able to wait
25 Relative
28 Worry or care
29 Small-time criminal
31 Tastes good
32 Thinking of what will benefit others
33 Identified

DOWN
1 Temporary care
2 Shining, beaming, giving off rays
4 Attack or invasion, sometimes to uncover something illegal
5 Lightly or gently pushed
6 Nervously moving about or twitching
7 Not necessarily bad, but a trouble-maker
9 Started; induced
12 Attitude of being not thankful
14 Charitable, usually religious, house for helping needy people
16 Having the effect of putting one in a trance or asleep
18 Small in size
19 Illness causing difficulty breathing
21 Particularly
23 Put up with; endure
24 Lecturing; reprimanding
26 Short pants
27 Ate quickly and completely or hungrily
30 Carried

VOCABULARY CROSSWORD ANSWER KEY
Bud, Not Buddy

VOCABULARY WORKSHEET 1 - *Bud, Not Buddy*

____ 1. RAID   A. Carried

____ 2. TEMPERATURE   B. Chose

____ 3. CONCLUSIONS   C. Hardship; giving up something

____ 4. VENTRILOQUIST   D. Wary, not trusting

____ 5. NUDGED   E. Easy to see

____ 6. ESPECIALLY   F. Lightly or gently pushed

____ 7. FUMBLING   G. Hotness or coldness

____ 8. LUGGED   H. Proper

____ 9. TEMPORARY   I. Repeatedly demanded

____10. ORNERY   J. A made-up name usually assumed to hide one's true identity

____11. DECIDED   K. Person who doesn't eat meat

____12. PROVOKED   L. Thinking of what will benefit others

____13. SUSPICIOUS   M. Clumsily searching

____14. OBVIOUS   N. Attack or invasion, sometimes to uncover something illegal

____15. ILK   O. Not necessarily bad, but a trouble-maker

____16. VERMIN   P. Act of God; something impossible happens

____17. COPACETIC   Q. Performer who can make the voice appear to come from somewhere else

____18. MIRACLE   R. Low life creatures like rats

____19. REPUTATION   S. A person's character observed by others

____20. INSISTED   T. Short pants

____21. KNICKERS   U. Started; induced

____22. CONSIDERATE   V. Particularly

____23. ALIAS   W. Kind, group, set

____24. VEGETARIAN   X. Results, decisions, deductions

____25. SACRIFICE   Y. Not permanent; just for a while

KEY: VOCABULARY WORKSHEET 1 - *Bud, Not Buddy*

N	1. RAID	A. Carried
G	2. TEMPERATURE	B. Chose
X	3. CONCLUSIONS	C. Hardship; giving up something
Q	4. VENTRILOQUIST	D. Wary, not trusting
F	5. NUDGED	E. Easy to see
V	6. ESPECIALLY	F. Lightly or gently pushed
M	7. FUMBLING	G. Hotness or coldness
A	8. LUGGED	H. Proper
Y	9. TEMPORARY	I. Repeatedly demanded
O	10. ORNERY	J. A made-up name usually assumed to hide one's true identity
B	11. DECIDED	K. Person who doesn't eat meat
U	12. PROVOKED	L. Thinking of what will benefit others
D	13. SUSPICIOUS	M. Clumsily searching
E	14. OBVIOUS	N. Attack or invasion, sometimes to uncover something illegal
W	15. ILK	O. Not necessarily bad, but a trouble-maker
R	16. VERMIN	P. Act of God; something impossible happens
H	17. COPACETIC	Q. Performer who can make the voice appear to come from somewhere else
P	18. MIRACLE	R. Low life creatures like rats
S	19. REPUTATION	S. A person's character observed by others
I	20. INSISTED	T. Short pants
T	21. KNICKERS	U. Started; induced
L	22. CONSIDERATE	V. Particularly
J	23. ALIAS	W. Kind, group, set
K	24. VEGETARIAN	X. Results, decisions, deductions
C	25. SACRIFICE	Y. Not permanent; just for a while

VOCABULARY WORKSHEET 2 - *Bud, Not Buddy*

___ 1. Lightly or gently pushed
A. NUDGED   B. SACRIFICED   C. ILKED   D. LUGGED

___ 2. A person's character observed by others
A. VERMIN   B. MIRACLE   C. REPUTATION   D. KIN

___ 3. Proper
A. COPACETIC   B. SUSPICIOUS   C. DELICIOUS   D. KIN

___ 4. Illness causing difficulty breathing
A. COPACETIC   B. KNICKERS   C. ASTHMA   D. ILK

___ 5. Repeatedly demanded
A. TOLERATED   B. PROVOKED   C. RECOGNIZED   D. INSISTED

___ 6. Act of God; something impossible happens
A. RAID   B. MIRACLE   C. VERMIN   D. MIDGET

___ 7. Relative
A. GLUM   B. KIN   C. ILK   D. VERMIN

___ 8. Attitude of being not thankful
A. COPACETIC   B. INGRATITUDE   C. PATIENT   D. PROVOKED

___ 9. Put up with; endure
A. RECOGNIZE   B. TOLERATE   C. SACRIFICE   D. PROVOKE

___ 10. Hardship; giving up something
A. MIRACLE   B. INGRATITUDE   C. SACRIFICE   D. FOSTER

___ 11. Chose
A. INSISTED   B. NUDGED   C. TOLERATED   D. DECIDED

___ 12. Thinking of what will benefit others
A. PATIENT   B. HOODLUM   C. CONSIDERATE   D. SACRIFICING

___ 13. Recognize something's value
A. TOLERATE   B. FOSTER   C. APPRECIATE   D. ALIAS

___ 14. Low life creatures like rats
A. VERMIN   B. CONCLUSIONS   C. ILKS   D. VEGETARIANS

___ 15. Tastes good
A. DELICIOUS   B. RADIATING   C. DEVOURED   D. SUSPICIOUS

VOCABULARY WORKSHEET 2 ANSWER KEY *Bud, Not Buddy*

A 1. Lightly or gently pushed
   A. NUDGED   B. SACRIFICED   C. ILKED   D. LUGGED

C 2. A person's character observed by others
   A. VERMIN   B. MIRACLE   C. REPUTATION   D. KIN

A 3. Proper
   A. COPACETIC   B. SUSPICIOUS   C. DELICIOUS   D. KIN

C 4. Illness causing difficulty breathing
   A. COPACETIC   B. KNICKERS   C. ASTHMA   D. ILK

D 5. Repeatedly demanded
   A. TOLERATED   B. PROVOKED   C. RECOGNIZED   D. INSISTED

B 6. Act of God; something impossible happens
   A. RAID   B. MIRACLE   C. VERMIN   D. MIDGET

B 7. Relative
   A. GLUM   B. KIN   C. ILK   D. VERMIN

B 8. Attitude of being not thankful
   A. COPACETIC   B. INGRATITUDE   C. PATIENT   D. PROVOKED

B 9. Put up with; endure
   A. RECOGNIZE   B. TOLERATE   C. SACRIFICE   D. PROVOKE

C 10. Hardship; giving up something
   A. MIRACLE   B. INGRATITUDE   C. SACRIFICE   D. FOSTER

D 11. Chose
   A. INSISTED   B. NUDGED   C. TOLERATED   D. DECIDED

C 12. Thinking of what will benefit others
   A. PATIENT   B. HOODLUM   C. CONSIDERATE   D. SACRIFICING

C 13. Recognize something's value
   A. TOLERATE   B. FOSTER   C. APPRECIATE   D. ALIAS

A 14. Low life creatures like rats
   A. VERMIN   B. CONCLUSIONS   C. ILKS   D. VEGETARIANS

A 15. Tastes good
   A. DELICIOUS   B. RADIATING   C. DEVOURED   D. SUSPICIOUS

VOCABULARY JUGGLE LETTER REVIEW GAME 1 *Bud, Not Buddy*

1. QLIVTOTRESNIU = 1. V_____
   Performer who can make the voice appear to come from somewhere else

2. IDRA = 2. R_____
   Attack or invasion, sometimes to uncover something illegal

3. AILEPYESCL = 3. E_____
   Particularly

4. RORTMYPEA = 4. T_____
   Not permanent; just for a while

5. ILNFMGUB = 5. F_____
   Clumsily searching

6. GDLUGE = 6. L_____
   Carried

7. CALMIER = 7. M_____
   Act of God; something impossible happens

8. FICSCERAI = 8. S_____
   Hardship; giving up something

9. EYORNR = 9. O_____
   Not necessarily bad, but a trouble-maker

10. RDTCNEESOIA =10. C_____
    Thinking of what will benefit others

11. ISOMINS =11. M_____
    Charitable, usually religious, house for helping needy people

12. GTMIDE =12. M_____
    Small in size

13. TTDIGIERNAU =13. I_____
    Attitude of being not thankful

14. ICUSSSPUIO =14. S_____
    Wary, not trusting

15. TRFOSE =15. F_____
    Temporary care

16. RUNTRGTOI =16. T_____
    Mistreating; tormenting; abusing

17. RUEDVDEO =17. D_____
    Ate quickly and completely or hungrily

18. ARTTLEOE =18. T_____
    Put up with; endure

19. MNVERI =19. V_____
    Low life creatures like rats

20. OIUPESRC =20. P_____
    Valuable

VOCABULARY JUGGLE LETTER REVIEW GAME 1 ANSWER KEY *Bud, Not Buddy*

1. QLIVTOTRESNIU = **1. VENTRILOQUIST**
   Performer who can make the voice appear to come from somewhere else

2. IDRA = **2. RAID**
   Attack or invasion, sometimes to uncover something illegal

3. AILEPYESCL = **3. ESPECIALLY**
   Particularly

4. RORTMYPEA = **4. TEMPORARY**
   Not permanent; just for a while

5. ILNFMGUB = **5. FUMBLING**
   Clumsily searching

6. GDLUGE = **6. LUGGED**
   Carried

7. CALMIER = **7. MIRACLE**
   Act of God; something impossible happens

8. FICSCERAI = **8. SACRIFICE**
   Hardship; giving up something

9. EYORNR = **9. ORNERY**
   Not necessarily bad, but a trouble-maker

10. RDTCNEESOIA = **10. CONSIDERATE**
    Thinking of what will benefit others

11. ISOMINS = **11. MISSION**
    Charitable, usually religious, house for helping needy people

12. GTMIDE = **12. MIDGET**
    Small in size

13. TTDIGIERNAU = **13. INGRATITUDE**
    Attitude of being not thankful

14. ICUSSSPUIO = **14. SUSPICIOUS**
    Wary, not trusting

15. TRFOSE = **15. FOSTER**
    Temporary care

16. RUNTRGTOI = **16. TORTURING**
    Mistreating; tormenting; abusing

17. RUEDVDEO = **17. DEVOURED**
    Ate quickly and completely or hungrily

18. ARTTLEOE = **18. TOLERATE**
    Put up with; endure

19. MNVERI = **19. VERMIN**
    Low life creatures like rats

20. OIUPESRC = **20. PRECIOUS**
    Valuable

VOCABULARY JUGGLE LETTER REVIEW GAME 2 *Bud, Not Buddy*

1. NUIRETTGADI = 1. I_____
   Attitude of being not thankful

2. SALAI = 2. A_____
   A made-up name usually assumed to hide one's true identity

3. REPODOKV = 3. P_____
   Started; induced

4. OACSEDRNITE = 4. C_____
   Thinking of what will benefit others

5. RONYER = 5. O_____
   Not necessarily bad, but a trouble-maker

6. EAVENIAGTR = 6. V_____
   Person who doesn't eat meat

7. ELGDGU = 7. L_____
   Carried

8. EORUNIAPTT = 8. R_____
   A person's character observed by others

9. ONTTGIURR = 9. T_____
   Mistreating; tormenting; abusing

10. ENDDGU = 10. N_____
    Lightly or gently pushed

11. DRAI = 11. R_____
    Attack or invasion, sometimes to uncover something illegal

12. KIL = 12. I_____
    Kind, group, set

13. PTAREACPEI = 13. A_____
    Recognize something's value

14. RUPESIOC = 14. P_____
    Valuable

15. AIMRLMNTIAO = 15. M_____
    Relating to marriage

16. UNFMGLIB = 16. F_____
    Clumsily searching

17. OTTLERAE = 17. T_____
    Put up with; endure

18. IVRNME = 18. V_____
    Low life creatures like rats

19. UHOMDOL = 19. H_____
    Small-time criminal

20. NKI = 20. K_____
    Relative

VOCABULARY JUGGLE LETTER REVIEW GAME 2 ANSWER KEY *Bud, Not Buddy*

1. NUIRETTGADI = **1. INGRATITUDE**
   Attitude of being not thankful
2. SALAI = **2. ALIAS**
   A made-up name usually assumed to hide one's true identity
3. REPODOKV = **3. PROVOKED**
   Started; induced
4. OACSEDRNITE = **4. CONSIDERATE**
   Thinking of what will benefit others
5. RONYER = **5. ORNERY**
   Not necessarily bad, but a trouble-maker
6. EAVENIAGTR = **6. VEGETARIAN**
   Person who doesn't eat meat
7. ELGDGU = **7. LUGGED**
   Carried
8. EORUNIAPTT = **8. REPUTATION**
   A person's character observed by others
9. ONTTGIURR = **9. TORTURING**
   Mistreating; tormenting; abusing
10. ENDDGU = **10. NUDGED**
    Lightly or gently pushed
11. DRAI = **11. RAID**
    Attack or invasion, sometimes to uncover something illegal
12. KIL = **12. ILK**
    Kind, group, set
13. PTAREACPEI = **13. APPRECIATE**
    Recognize something's value
14. RUPESIOC = **14. PRECIOUS**
    Valuable
15. AIMRLMNTIAO = **15. MATRIMONIAL**
    Relating to marriage
16. UNFMGLIB = **16. FUMBLING**
    Clumsily searching
17. OTTLERAE = **17. TOLERATE**
    Put up with; endure
18. IVRNME = **18. VERMIN**
    Low life creatures like rats
19. UHOMDOL = **19. HOODLUM**
    Small-time criminal
20. NKI = **20. KIN**
    Relative

VOCABULARY WORD LIST Bud, Not Buddy

No.	Word	Clue/Definition
1.	ALIAS	A made-up name usually assumed to hide one's true identity
2.	APPRECIATE	Recognize something's value
3.	ASTHMA	Illness causing difficulty breathing
4.	CONCERN	Worry or care
5.	CONCLUSIONS	Results, decisions, deductions
6.	CONSIDERATE	Thinking of what will benefit others
7.	COPACETIC	Proper
8.	DECIDED	Chose
9.	DELICIOUS	Tastes good
10.	DEVOURED	Ate quickly and completely or hungrily
11.	ESPECIALLY	Particularly
12.	FIDGETING	Nervously moving about or twitching
13.	FOSTER	Temporary care
14.	FUMBLING	Clumsily searching
15.	GLUM	Sad
16.	HOODLUM	Small-time criminal
17.	HYPNOTIZING	Having the effect of putting one in a trance or asleep
18.	ILK	Kind, group, set
19.	INGRATITUDE	Attitude of being not thankful
20.	INSISTED	Repeatedly demanded
21.	KIN	Relative
22.	KNICKERS	Short pants
23.	LUGGED	Carried
24.	MATRIMONIAL	Relating to marriage
25.	MIDGET	Small in size
26.	MIRACLE	Act of God; something impossible happens
27.	MISSION	Charitable, usually religious, house for helping needy people
28.	NUDGED	Lightly or gently pushed
29.	OBVIOUS	Easy to see
30.	ORNERY	Not necessarily bad, but a trouble-maker
31.	PATIENT	Able to wait
32.	PRECIOUS	Valuable
33.	PROVOKED	Started; induced
34.	RADIATING	Shining, beaming, giving off rays
35.	RAID	Attack or invasion, sometimes to uncover something illegal
36.	RECOGNIZED	Identified
37.	REPUTATION	A person's character observed by others
38.	SACRIFICE	Hardship; giving up something
39.	SCOLDING	Lecturing; reprimanding
40.	SUSPICIOUS	Wary, not trusting
41.	TEMPERATURE	Hotness or coldness
42.	TEMPORARY	Not permanent; just for a while
43.	TOLERATE	Put up with; endure
44.	TORTURING	Mistreating; tormenting; abusing
45.	VEGETARIAN	Person who doesn't eat meat
46.	VENTRILOQUIST	Performer who can make the voice appear to come from somewhere else
47.	VERMIN	Low life creatures like rats